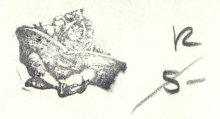

R
5-
250

Macroeconomics and Micropolitics

D0143828

Macro-economics

& Micro-politics

★ ★ ★ ★ ★ ★ ★ ★ ★ ★ ★ ★ ★ ★ ★

The Electoral Effects of Economic Issues

D. Roderick Kiewiet

The University of Chicago Press
Chicago & London

The University of Chicago Press, Chicago 60637
The University of Chicago Press, Ltd., London

©1983 by The University of Chicago
All rights reserved. Published 1983
Paperback edition 1984
Printed in the United States of America

93 92 91 90 89 88 87 86 85 84   5 4 3 2

Library of Congress Cataloging in Publication Data
Kiewiet, D. Roderick.
  Macroeconomics and micropolitics.
  A revision of the author's thesis (Ph.D.)—Yale University.
  Includes bibliographical references and index.
  1. Elections—United States.   2. Inflation (Finance)
—United States—Public opinion.   3. Unemployment—
United States—Public opinion.   4. Public opinion—
United States.   I. Title.
JK1967.K53   1983   324.973   82-21985
ISBN 0-226-43532-6 (cloth)
ISBN 0-226-43533-4 (paper)

Contents

To my Grandmother, Hermine Bergman (1911-1981)

Acknowledgments

This book grew directly out of the doctoral dissertation I wrote at Yale University. I would like to thank several people there who helped me immeasurably by providing generous amounts of advice, commentary, and criticism: above all, my advisor, Donald R. Kinder; my teachers David Cameron, Paul Johnson, Gerald Kramer, Robert Lane, David Mayhew, Steve Rosenstone, and Edward Tufte; my fellow graduate students Jim Austin, Jay Budzizewski, Tom Cavanagh, Jennifer Hochschild, John Morgan, Joe Morone, and Harold Stanley; and my wife Lorraine. I would also like to thank Sandy Aivano for her help in programming and computing, and Yale University for its generous financial aid during my years in graduate school.

During the last few years I have also benefited from extensive discussions of this research with my colleagues at Caltech, especially Bob Bates, Bruce Cain, John Ferejohn, Morris Fiorina, and Roger Noll. I am also indebted to Richard Brody, Ben Page, and David Sears for their valuable comments and criticism. Finally, I would like to thank Barbara Calli for a superb job of word processing and Carl Lydick for his valuable assistance in preparing this book for publication.

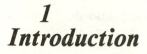

1
Introduction

In the last several years dozens of public opinion polls have shown economic problems to be the major source of public concern. This is hardly surprising, given the erratic performance of the nation's economy during this period. But even in the midst of prosperity such worries are never too far from the surface: when asked in a 1964 survey to name their fondest hopes and worst fears—for themselves and for the country as a whole—Americans referred to economic matters more frequently than to anything else.[1] For better or for worse, economic concerns occupy a central place in American life.

Economic concerns occupy a central place in American political life as well. Most accounts of U.S. history stress the strong influence the long periods of growth and prosperity, as well as the numerous panics and depressions, have had upon the course of national politics—especially elections. With the expansion in the size and scope of government during this century there has surely been a concomitant increase in the electoral importance of the economy. Few would deny, of course, that voters take other, noneconomic factors into account; moral and cultural issues, foreign policy positions, or a candidate's character (or lack thereof) often come into play in election campaigns. But as most pundits and politicians see it, when voters step into the booth, it is ultimately "bread and butter" economic concerns which determine which lever they will pull.

Until recently, knowledge about just exactly how economic issues affected voting behavior was largely confined to the domain of political folk wisdom. However, the troubled economy of the last decade has captured the attention of political scientists as well as the public, and there has been a veritable explosion of theory and research in this area. To be sure, the relationship between the economy and the political system is not a one-way street—several studies have dealt with the influences of political considerations upon economic policymaking and macroeconomic outcomes.[2] This book, however, will focus on relationships running in the opposite direction. More specifically, it will investigate the effects of economic concerns upon the decisions made by individual voters in American national elections.

This study builds upon a large and extensive literature; as suggested above, dozens of books and articles examining the electoral impact of a wide range of economic variables have appeared in the last few years. These studies range from analyses of several decades of national voting and economic statistics to intensive examinations of survey data from a single election. None have employed exactly the same set of assumptions or the same statistical models. Yet one can identify two basic dimensions running through this body of research. The first concerns voters' decision rules. According to the *incumbency-oriented* hypothesis, voters respond to all manner of economic adversity by tending to vote against the incumbent office-holders, and to any sort of economic improvement by tending to vote for them. An alternative hypothesis is that voting is *policy-oriented*; it holds that voters choose between candidates for national office on the basis of differences in the relative macroeconomic priorities of the respective parties. In particular, voters who are concerned about unemployment give greater support to Democratic candidates, while those who are relatively more averse to inflation tend to vote Republican.

A second basic dimension concerns the weight voters assign to different types of economic events, experiences, and information. As before, two general alternatives have emerged from previous theory and research. The first, the *personal experiences* hypothesis, posits that voters react mainly to immediate, directly experienced economic conditions. According to the second, the *national assessments* hypothesis, it is instead their perceptions and evaluations of the nation's economy which lead them to choose one candidate over another. These two alternatives can be considered in conjunction with the two decision rule alternatives, resulting in personal experiences and national assessments versions of both incumbency-oriented and policy-oriented voting. A voter's decision to vote Democratic instead of Republican, for example, could grow out of the experience of joblessness, or from the conviction that unemployment is a serious problem for the country as a whole. The resultant four hypotheses, it should be added, are not mutually exclusive. Evidence about one, either supportive or nonsupportive, does not necessarily imply anything about any of the others.

This book, then, will examine voting in American presidential and congressional elections in terms of this two-dimensional (incumbency-oriented or policy-oriented, personal experiences or national assessments) framework. It will thus constitute a considerably more comprehensive and systematic investigation of the electoral effects of economic issues than has so far been conducted. For although this framework for analysis was abstracted from a sizable collection of previous studies, none of these studies considered more than one of these dimensions or pair of alternatives. Moreover, this research program has given far less attention to some areas than to others. In particular, only a handful of studies have focused upon either the personal experiences or national assessments versions of the policy-oriented hypothesis; most have dealt only with incumbency-oriented voting. A major contribution of this study will be to at least start to address this imbalance.

Another important contribution will be to generate some badly needed side evidence on the various hypotheses. In public opinion/voting behavior research, as in quantitative social science generally, the findings generated by a single piece of analysis are rarely very conclusive. Measurement errors, specification errors, and spurious associations pose an ever-present threat. Even when one is sure that findings are genuine, it is usually easy to come up with alternative explanations for them. But any hypothesis is usually based upon a number of theoretical premises and assumptions, and in turn spawns some number of corollary hypotheses. When empirical support for a particular hypothesis is coupled with empirical support for the assumptions it is based upon, and when several related predictions are also borne out in the data, confidence that findings mean what one thinks they mean rises dramatically.

The outline of this book is reasonably straightforward, and can be summarized quickly. Chapter 2 will examine previous work in this area in light of the two key dimensions upon which all subsequent analyses are based: Do voter's decisions reflect their direct personal encounters with economic problems, or from their perceptions that economic problems are troublesome for the nation as a whole? Second, is voting in response to economic concerns incumbency-oriented or policy-oriented? This chapter will identify the major theoretical strengths and weaknesses of the four specific hypotheses derived from this framework, and assess how well they have fared in previous research.

Chapter 3 will discuss the main problems entailed in estimating the electoral effects of economic concerns, and will develop some basic statistical models to be used in this task. Its concerns are thus more methodological than substantive.

Chapter 4 will investigate the personal experiences version of both the incumbency-oriented and policy-oriented hypotheses. The major share of this chapter will be devoted to reanalysis of previous studies in this area and reinterpretation of their findings. Chapter 5 will continue this line of inquiry by developing new and better indicators of personally encountered economic problems and by exploring the inferences voters make about these sorts of problems. The survey data on which these and all other analyses in this book are based come from the 1956-80 SRC-CPS National Election Studies. A few analyses will also employ data collected by various quarterly SRC-CPS Surveys of Consumer Finances.[3]

Chapter 6 will focus upon the national assessments version of the incumbency-oriented and policy-oriented hypotheses. Among other things, this chapter will also examine the relationship between individuals' personal economic experiences and their assessments of national economic problems. Chapter 7 will make some estimates of the aggregate electoral effects of these various economic concerns. The eighth and final chapter will recapitulate the major findings of this study, attempt to further account for them, and discuss the implications these findings have for our understanding of voting behavior and electoral competition.

2
Macroeconomics and
Micropolitics

Perhaps the most common observation made about elections in this country is that people "vote their pocketbooks." Indeed, in the minds of many students of American politics, the proposition that economic concerns powerfully influence voters' decisions enjoys the status of a self-evident truth. But like many self-evident truths, the assertion that people vote their pocketbooks provides little guidance in predicting just exactly how a given voter will vote in a particular election. This can be seen in a quick perusal of the early empirical studies of economic conditions and election results. These analyses entertained a large number of hypotheses: support for the more conservative party was held to be histori- cally associated with prosperity; drought-induced depressions in farm income were linked to increased support for the populists; the electoral success of the incumbent president was hypothesized to rise and fall with the business cycle; or the Republicans were seen to fare well in good times and poorly in bad times. More- over, the economic indicators used to explain different sets of electoral outcomes varied enormously, as did their conclusions as to the nature and strength of the politico-economic relationships they uncovered. In short, the general notion that economic condi- tions affect voting admits to a wide range of specific hypotheses.[1]

However, following publication in 1971 of Gerald Kramer's influential study, most subsequent research has focused on what will hereafter be referred to as the *incumbency-oriented* hypothesis.[2] (In this and in subsequent studies in this field, the status of incumbency is assigned to all candidates of the president's party; incumbents, then, include the incumbent president himself if he is running for reelection, his party's presidential nominee if he is not, and congressional candidates of his party.) This hypothesis posits that voters give greater support to the incumbents during periods of prosperity, but turn against them and opt for their opponents when times are poor. As Kramer acknowledged, the incumbency-oriented hypothesis was at least partly inspired by the work of Anthony Downs.[3] Voters, according to Downs, make their decisions under a high degree of uncertainty. Relevant information about the available choices, e.g., party platforms or campaign promises, is both bothersome to obtain and of questionable reliability. There is, however, one source of reliable information readily available to voters—the record of the incumbent administration. As Fiorina observes:

> Citizens are not fools. Having often observed political equivocation, if not outright lying, should they listen carefully to campaign promises? Having heard the economic, educational, sociological, defense, and foreign policy expert advisors disagree on both the effects of past policies and the prospects of future ones, should they pay close attention to policy debates? Even if concerned and competent, citizens appear to have little solid basis on which to cast their votes, save on those rare occasions when candidates take clear and differing positions on salient specific issues (e.g. busing, abortion, the Equal Rights Amendment).
>
> But are the citizens' choices actually so unclear? After all, they typically have one comparatively hard bit of data: they know what life has been like during the incumbent's administration. They need not know the precise economic or foreign policies of the incumbent administration in order to see or feel the results of those policies.[4]

As developed by Downs, Kramer, Fiorina, and others, the incumbency-oriented hypothesis has three central features. First, incumbency-oriented voting is seen to be *retrospective*—voters pay heed to what has occurred under the present incumbents, not to parties' or candidates' promises about the future.[5] Second, the hypothesis holds that voters are more familiar with and concerned about the *results* produced by public policy than with the specific policy instruments themselves. As Fiorina puts it, "I suspect that people generally are not terribly concerned about whether the government fights unemployment via public-works projects, tax rebates, or business tax credits. Whatever succeeds." This, of course, is the bottom line in Popkin and his associates' argument about the importance of the "competence factor" in elections. As their analysis of the 1972 presidential election demonstrated, the American voter often "cares less about which candidate is the closest to his ideal position on issues for which he has information and preferences, but cares most about which candidate can *deliver* the most."[6] Third, the actual decision rule posited by the hypothesis is very simple: If something good occurs, give the incumbents credit for it; if something bad occurs, blame them for it. When it comes to economic conditions, the incumbent president and candidates of his party will fare well electorally to the extent they preside over high employment, rapid growth, and low inflation. To the extent they do not, their support at the polls will erode.[7]

Most aggregate level time series analyses of U.S. economic and voting data, including Kramer's, have produced findings quite supportive of the incumbency-oriented hypothesis. Kramer's analysis of congressional elections from 1896 through 1964 clearly indicated that the American electorate rewards congressional candidates of the incumbent president's party during periods of prosperity, but turns against them and opts for their challengers during poor times. In this and in several other studies which corroborate Kramer's findings, change in per capita real disposable income over the course of the election year has been the best predictor of the incumbent party's electoral fortunes.[8]

An Alternative Hypothesis

The incumbency-oriented hypothesis obviously has a great deal going for it: it has a strong theoretical basis and has held up well under empirical scrutiny. It seems extremely doubtful, however, that in accounting for the electoral effects of economic concerns it is the whole story. Certainly voters prefer good economic conditions to bad. But prosperity is not all of one piece, and it is simply not possible for policymakers to attack all economic problems with equal fervor. In particular, the key question in economic policy during the past several years has been how much priority to assign to reducing unemployment versus reducing inflation. To be sure, the classic Phillips curve relationship between the two has deteriorated. There has been a steady increase in the underlying rate of inflation since the mid-1960s, and on a number of occasions the United States has experienced simultaneously high and rising rates of both inflation and unemployment. But it is still the case that medicine for one is usually bane for the other: policies to reduce unemployment typically do so by seeking to stimulate aggregate demand, while policies to lower inflation typically seek to depress aggregate demand. As Hibbs puts it:

> Although there is no fixed, stable trade-off between unemployment and inflation in the macro-economy, most economists and politicians recognize that full employment and price stability pose conflicting goals in the sense that it is difficult to make substantial progress on one problem without running risks with respect to the other.[9]

Furthermore, over the past three decades the major political parties have differed in the priority they assign to reducing inflation versus lowering unemployment. Compared to Republican administrations, Democratic administrations have been more sensitive to unemployment, and have been relatively more willing to risk some inflation to reduce it. Compared to Democratic administrations, though, Republican administrations have usually tolerated considerably more slack in the economy and thus unemployment to fight inflation. It seems quite reasonable to suspect, therefore, that voting in response to economic conditions is often *policy-oriented*: voters will tend to give greater support to Democratic presidential and congressional candidates during periods of high unemployment, but greater support to Republicans during inflationary periods. Instead of simply blaming the incumbents for any and all forms of economic difficulty, policy-oriented voters support the party which places a higher priority on attacking the particular economic problem that they are concerned about—whether or not that party is currently in power.

So construed, the policy-oriented hypothesis demands little more of voters than the incumbency-oriented hypothesis. It, too, holds that voters' decisions are retrospective in nature, weighing heavily their experiences of the recent past. Furthermore, policy-oriented voters also need only be concerned about the actual results of macroeconomic policies. They need not have a sophisticated understanding of fiscal and monetary policy instruments. Nor must they believe anything in particular about the nature of the relationship between inflation and unemployment. Rather, policy-oriented voting requires only that voters (1) see either inflation or unemployment as a serious problem and want to see it alleviated, and (2) that they perceive differences between the parties in the amount of effort and/or skill they would apply in combatting that problem.

There are a few important objections which might be lodged against the policy-oriented hypothesis. One might legitimately wonder, first of all, whether or not differences in the major parties' economic priorities are big enough for voters to pick up. To be sure, the extent to which voters perceive such differences is an empirical matter which the analyses in this book will frequently confront. It is clear, though, that politicians are not always helpful in this regard. During the last two presidential campaigns challengers Carter and Reagan both assaulted their incumbent opponents with the charge that they had presided over an unconscionable rise in the "misery index," a figure arrived at by simply summing the inflation and unemployment rates. Furthermore, a large body of political theory posits that candidates have incentives to blur and equivocate. Page's theory of political ambiguity, for example, holds that "the self-interest of politicians dictates that they avoid specific stands and limit themselves to vague actions and utterances."[10]

Political scientists, however, have had little trouble discerning differences between the major parties' stated policy priorities. True, there is plenty of fuzzing and hedging; challengers freely criticize any and all aspects of the incumbent's record, and incumbents, reluctant to admit to possible policy tradeoffs, either claim everything has improved under their tenure or that their opponents would only make things worse. But after analyzing a vast number of presidential statements, speeches, and party campaign platforms, Tufte concluded:

> It is clear that even what many consider to be the ideologically bland political parties of the United States display the classic differences between Left and Right on fundamental issues of economic policy—the distribution of

wealth and income, the proper scope and cost of government, and the trade-off between inflation and unemployment.[11]

Evidence derived from platforms and speeches, though, is not terribly persuasive. As indicated earlier, the policy-oriented hypothesis is much stronger theoretically if it requires voters to be concerned only about the actual results of economic policies. Differences in the parties' words can be quickly discounted if there are no differences in their behavior in office.

Again, political scientists have detected such differences in macroeconomic outcomes, at least with regard to unemployment. Hibbs's sophisticated time series analysis of quarterly unemployment rates indicated that Democratic administrations tended to push unemployment downward, while Republicans tended to allow it to rise.[12] However, no studies of comparable rigor have come forward claiming to detect similar performance differences with regard to inflation. Simple inspection of the Consumer Price Index time series certainly doesn't turn them up. Rather, starting with Eisenhower and ending with Carter, the average rate of inflation has been higher under each successive president than it was under his predecessor.

Of course, comparisons of inflation rates across administrations in office at different points in time are not necessarily very enlightening as to the nature and extent of differences in macroeconomic policy outcomes. Obviously unemployment and inflation are strongly affected by factors over which policymakers, at least in the short run, have no real control. Their room to maneuver is often quite limited. But this also means that the economy facing Republican administrations in the 1970s was very different from that facing the Democrats in the 1960s.[13] Were the present administration's policies to achieve results in line with their most optimistic forecasts, inflation during the next few years would average around 5 or 6% annually. This is far higher than the rate during the mid-1960s. Yet is there anyone who would claim that Ronald Reagan is a less enthusiastic inflation fighter than was Lyndon Johnson? For there to be real and important differences between the major parties, then, requires only that at a given moment, facing the same economy, a Republican administration would drive inflation down to a lower rate, and tolerate a higher unemployment rate in doing so, than would a Democratic administration.

Still, the empirical point remains—do *voters* actually perceive differences between the parties in the amount of effort and/or skill they apply in battling inflation and unemployment? Again, real and important differences between the parties need not be manifested in simple cross-time, cross-administration differences in inflation and unemployment rates, and thus such differences are not required for policy-oriented voting to make sense. But the incidence and strength of policy-oriented voting may well depend upon whether or not such differences exist and how big they are. If changing the party in power does lead to substantial changes in the expected direction in inflation and unemployment rates, party differences would be easier to pick up and undoubtedly be considered more important. As indicated earlier, time series analyses have been much more successful in finding differences between Republican and Democratic administrations on the unemployment front than in their performance vis-à-vis inflation. If voters are like political scientists, perhaps they too have generally detected larger party differences on unemployment than on inflation. Whatever the case, voters' perceptions of party differences are a crucial matter which this book will address on a number of occasions.

Ironically, an analysis of incumbency-oriented and policy-oriented voting would be severely compromised if the macroeconomic policies of Republican and Democratic administrations produced outcomes which were *too* divergent. Writing in the early 1970s, Arthur Okun observed:

> When the chips were down, the Democrats have taken
> their chances on inflation and the Republicans on unem-
> ployment and recession. For a generation, every major
> mistake in economic policy under a Democratic president
> has taken the form of overstimulating the economy and
> every major mistake under a Republican president of over-
> restraining it.[14]

If this were completely true, every jump in unemployment would occur under a Republican and every serious bout of inflation would occur under a Democrat. In the first case, the incumbency-oriented hypothesis predicts that voters will tend to vote against an incumbent Republican for running up unemployment because he is the incumbent; the policy-oriented hypothesis predicts that they will tend to vote against him because he is a

Republican. In the second case, the incumbency-oriented hypothesis predicts that voters will tend to punish the incumbent Democrat for running up inflation because he is the incumbent; the policy-oriented hypothesis predicts the same behavior, but because he is a Democrat. In neither case can policy-oriented voting be distinguished from incumbency-oriented voting.

There appears, though, to be enough variation in economic conditions during the period under scrutiny (1956-1980) to disentangle incumbency-oriented from policy-oriented voting. Despite the genuine differences in their relative priorities, Republican and Democratic administrations alike have presided over times of both low and high unemployment, and periods of mild increases in prices as well as galloping inflation. It should be noted, though, that much of this variation occurred in the years after Okun made his observation. This is especially true on the down side. Luckily for this analysis (and unluckily for everyone else), since 1972 we have seen two Republican presidents plagued by inflation, and a Democrat in office during a sharp jump in unemployment.

This discussion suggests another problem with the policy-oriented hypothesis: it would seem to present those in power with perverse incentives. It appears to imply, paradoxically, that when in office the Republicans could help themselves by allowing a high rate of inflation, while the Democrats could bolster their reelection chances by running up a high unemployment rate. To some extent such a strategy is probably often tempting, for the hypothesis does suggest that a given increase in unemployment would hurt a Republican incumbent worse than a Democratic one, while a given increase in inflation would prove more harmful to a Democrat than to a Republican.[15] And certainly there is always a greater or lesser degree of tension between a president and the more extreme elements of his party. Nixon and Ford, for example, probably went somewhat farther to alleviate unemployment than many of the Republican faithful liked, and Carter clearly worried more about inflation than did those in the liberal wing of his party.

However, an incumbent party's strategy of deliberately exacerbating the economic problem it is supposed to be more adept at handling (or, less flagrantly, of attempting to protect a weak electoral flank by shifting into a vigorous attack on the problem it is supposed to be relatively less adept at handling) would almost certainly be counterproductive. A complete flip-flop on macroeconomic policy priorities would not only betray the party's key constituent groups and alienate some of its most dependable supporters, but the resultant uncertainty as to what the party could be expected to do in office would frighten away many others.[16] Furthermore, it would be trading in valuable political capital for a very questionable short-run gain. As Okun pointed out, a party's long-term favorable image would surely be eroded by such policy failures. Any perception of the Republican party as more committed to fighting inflation, for example, would inevitably fade in the face of a Republican administration which apparently tolerated a high rate of inflation.[17]

To be sure, the previous Democratic administration seems to have adopted this strategy. President Carter fully supported the Federal Reserve's credit-tightening moves, which helped trigger the 1980 recession. The argument here, though, is not that the Democrats care only about unemployment and pay no heed to inflation, while the Republicans are prepared to accept any rate of unemployment for the sake of price stability. It is, rather, that the parties' *relative* priorities differ, and this point seems secure. Even though Carter may have opted for typically "Republican" policies in the face of a rapid surge in inflation, the record of Reagan's first two years in office indicates that he is hardly less zealous than Carter in the battle against inflation, or more troubled by unemployment.

Previous Research on Policy-oriented Voting

Unlike the incumbency-oriented hypothesis, the policy-oriented hypothesis has not been subjected to a large amount of empirical testing. The only analysis of aggregate time series data (1896-1972) to consider it explicitly was that of Goodman and Kramer. This study was actually a reestimation of a model developed by Arcelus and Meltzer, and contained a number of features they found undesirable.[18] Still, their results provided some support for the policy-oriented hypothesis, at least on the unemployment side: regardless of the party of the incumbent president, the electorate gave greater support to Democratic congressional candidates during periods of high unemployment. An analysis of recent presidential elections by Meltzer and Vellrath generated a similar pattern of findings.[19] Unlike previously cited studies, theirs utilized a pooled cross-section of state election returns (for president) from the 1960 through 1972 elections. But like Goodman and Kramer, they too found that high levels of unemployment benefited Democratic candidates. Estimates of the effects of income changes and inflation, in contrast, were generally in line with the incumbency-oriented hypothesis.

In short, these studies have afforded the unemployment side of the policy-oriented hypothesis some support. The inflation side, though, has not fared as well. Although these are pretty slender threads of evidence, the findings seem quite plausible in light of our earlier discussion. As previously noted, analyses by Hibbs, Sundquist, and others indicated that postwar Democratic administrations do appear to have generated lower unemployment rates, *ceteris paribus*, than Republican administrations; inflation, in contrast, has simply kept going up. It should be remembered, though, that evidence of the electorate giving greater support to Democratic candidates during periods of high unemployment (and the lack of evidence of the electorate turning to the Republicans during surges in inflation) comes from only a few studies. Thus these findings, though plausible, should be accepted as far more tentative than the vast body of evidence documenting incumbency-oriented voting.

Economic Concerns and Individual Voting Behavior

There are, then, two major alternative hypotheses about the effects of economic conditions upon voting in national elections. The incumbency-oriented hypothesis posits that voters give greater support to the incumbents when economic conditions are good, but turn against them and opt for their challengers when conditions are poor. The policy-oriented alternative predicts that Democratic candidates will receive more support during times of high unemployment, while bouts of inflation lead to more support for the Republicans. The hypotheses have much in common—both see the electorate responding retrospectively to actual economic conditions. They differ mainly in the decision rule they specify. According to the first, voters make their decisions on the basis of how satisfactory economic conditions have been under the incumbent administration. The second holds instead that their choices reflect the relative economic priorities of the major political parties.

The studies discussed so far which have examined the two hypotheses also have a great deal in common. Virtually all were based upon time series data spanning several decades, and the data were of a highly aggregate nature—national vote shares won by a party's presidential nominees or, collectively, its congressional candidates, and national economic variables. Strictly speaking, this means that their findings hold for entire electorates, and should not be interpreted as illuminating the behavior of individual voters. Tufte makes this point quite succinctly:

> Many different models of the underlying electorate are consistent with electoral outcomes which are collectively rational; and the observation of aggregate rationality clearly does not imply a unique specification or description of individual voters or of groups of voters making up the electorate.[20]

In no way does this detract from the importance of the aggregate level studies; although the study of individual political behavior is in and of itself psychologically interesting, it is not politically very interesting unless there is reason to believe that it adds up to something which has important consequences for the political system. Had economic conditions no effect on the outcomes of national elections, there would be little reason for political scientists to worry about precisely how economic conditions affect the choices made by individual voters.

Given the strong link between elections and the economy, though, the matter of just how various economic concerns affect individual voters' decisions becomes a very live issue. Obviously a good starting point is to determine how well their choices are explained by the incumbency-oriented and policy-oriented hypotheses. Evidence on these points, however, would shed no light on other extremely important facets of individual voting behavior. Above all, it would tell us little about the particular worries, perceptions, and evaluations concerning inflation, unemployment, or other economic problems which voters in American elections take into account.

So what exactly is the nature of the economic concerns which move a voter to choose one candidate over another? According to one of the most widely held assumptions about political behavior, the answer is simple—voting in response to unemployment, inflation, or more general economic concerns is the product of immediate, personally experienced conditions and events. This view of political behavior will henceforth be referred to as the *personal experiences* hypothesis. Adopting this perspective, personal experience versions of both the incumbency-oriented and policy-oriented hypotheses can be specified. Such a version of the former hypothesis would hold that those individuals whose recent economic fortunes have been favorable would tend to support the incumbents, while those whose fortunes have soured would tend to support the opposition. Thus the incumbent party falters at the polls during economic downturns because there are more voters encountering economic difficulties in their own lives. The personal experience version of the policy-oriented hypothesis would have it that it is those individuals who are themselves injured by or threatened with unemployment who identify with and vote for the party which has stressed action against unemployment, i.e., the Democrats. Similarly, those more advantaged and secure individuals who are less susceptible to unemployment tend to favor price stability and the Republican party.

The personal experiences hypothesis has enormous intuitive appeal. Few would dispute Adam Smith's observation that "every man feels his own pleasures and his own pains more sensibly than those of other people."[21] And any number of examples attesting to the political primacy of personal concerns and experiences leap quickly to mind. Thousands of people residing in the environs of JFK Airport blockade surrounding highways in protest against the Concorde, which, upon landing and taking off, would rattle their houses substantially more than other aircraft. Ron Kovic, wounded and paralyzed during the Tet Offensive, then relegated to the human scrap heap of Ward I-C, St. Alban's Naval Hospital, channels his rage into organizing the Vietnam Veterans Against the War.[22] Personal *economic* concerns, of course, are thought to be especially potent politically. Veterans, poor people, and farmers have at one time or another marched on Washington, protesting their economic plight and demanding more help from the government.

Besides the intuitive appeal of its fundamental egocentrism, this account is bolstered by other considerations. A second major reason to believe that individuals vote in response to immediate, personally experienced economic conditions is that the requisite information is picked up directly in their daily lives. As Popkin and his associates put it in expounding their "investment theory" of voting,

> Usable political information is acquired in the process of making individual economic decisions; housewives learn about inflation of retail prices; homebuyers find out the trends in mortgage loan interest rates, and owners of stocks follow the Dow-Jones averages.[23]

Opportunity costs associated with obtaining this sort of information are quite low. Although some information about the political world is still required, it is kept to a minimum. And the smaller the information demands made by a theory of voting behavior, the more plausible that theory is going to be. In his review of a generation of work in public opinion and voting behavior, Converse makes no bones about it: "Surely the most familiar fact to arise from sample surveys in all countries is that popular levels of information about public affairs are, from the point of view of the informed observer, astonishing low."[24]

This is true, he believes, because the world of politics is remote and peripheral to the life of the average citizen. When political issues do intrude into the citizen's day-to-day existence, however, it's a different story:

> When they are doorstep issues for large sections of the population, such as whether one's child or grandchild will be obliged to ride a bus to a distant school perceived as being less physically safe than the neighborhood one, then a vastly greater proportion of the population falls above the tilt point where attentiveness is galvanized.[25]

Unemployment, inflation, or economic concerns in general would seem to be classic "doorstep issues," wherein recent personal problems and experiences readily become "usable political information."

In recent years there has appeared a rash of analyses and arguments challenging Converse's characterization of the mass public as politically uninterested, inattentive, and uninformed. Most argue that his view is accurate only for the drowsily complacent Eisenhower years; over the course of the sixties, however, the mass public became more interested, more attentive, and thus more ideologically consistent in its political thinking. In no way, though, do these studies refute the proposition that immediate personal concerns are of primary political importance—on the contrary, it is often evoked to explain these putative changes in American political life. Nie, Verba, and Petrocik, for example, argue that the American voter has been changing because political issues "have come to have a more direct impact on daily life." There has occurred, they claim, a "penetration of issues into the life space of the citizenry."[26]

During the last few years a number of studies have examined the personal experiences hypothesis. As was true of the time series analyses, virtually all of them confined their attention to incumbency-oriented voting. In this case research efforts were probably guided as much by the availability of usable data as by the attractiveness of the personal experiences view of voting: since 1956 the biennial SRC-CPS National Election Studies have asked respondents the following question:

> We are interested in how people are getting along financially these days. Would you say that you (and your family) are better off or worse off financially than you were a year ago, or about the same?

Although these studies employed a wide range of statistical techniques, most of their findings were in broad agreement with each other. In most presidential elections, voters who felt their financial situation had recently worsened did tend to vote against the incumbent, while those who perceived their fortunes to be on the upswing tended to vote for him.[27] On the other hand, voters' perceptions of recent trends in their family's finances rarely appeared to have much of an impact upon their choices between congressional candidates,[28] nor did these perceptions seem to matter much in senatorial and gubernatorial elections.[29] This body of evidence, then, affords a very uneven measure of support for the personal experiences version of the incumbency-oriented hypothesis.

Few studies have directly examined this version of the policy-oriented hypothesis. There is, however, a massive literature which indirectly supports the contention that voting in response to personally experienced economic difficulties is policy-oriented. This is the research documenting the association between class cleavages and political parties' sources of electoral support: parties of the Left draw support disproportionately from lower-income, working-class groups; conversely, parties of the Right draw their support disproportionately from higher-income, middle-class groups.[30] The personal experiences version of the policy-oriented hypothesis provides a straightforward explanation for this pattern. People in lower-income and occupational status groups experience substantially higher unemployment rates, and thus (in this country) tend to vote more Democratic; individuals in the higher-income categories, in contrast, are touched by unemployment far less often and thus generally opt for price stability and the Republicans. When in office, then, parties simply pursue policies which favor their supporters—ergo, the Democrats battle unemployment while the Republicans attempt to hold the line on inflation.

This view certainly finds support in individual level data: Hibbs's analyses of several surveys led him to conclude that (consistent with their "objective class interests") "Low and middle income and occupational status groups are more averse to unemployment than inflation, whereas, upper income and occupational status groups are more concerned about inflation than unemployment."[31] Lerman expresses this interpretation of class voting quite clearly:

> The indicators of class simply segregate people into groups whose experiences with inflation, unemployment, real income growth, integration, the health care system, etc., are roughly the same. In this view it is not subjective class identification or position in the social system which influence political attitudes, but the information about the world the individual receives and his personal experiences in that world, and the indicators which we take as dividing people into classes only divide people into groups with similar information and experiences.[32]

In other words, class voting is accounted for by policy-oriented voting in response to personally experienced economic conditions. Obviously this is only one of several plausible inferences which can be made about the link between class membership and party support. But there also exists a fair amount of research linking personally experienced economic problems with policy preferences, at least with regard to unemployment. Schlozman and Verba's thorough and comprehensive analysis of the political consequences of joblessness found that currently unemployed respondents were, not surprisingly, more supportive of a number of policies designed to boost employment.[33] These findings are corroborated in studies by Kiewiet and Kinder and by Sears and his associates.[34]

More importantly, Schlozman and Verba also report a piece of direct evidence on voting. Their analysis of data from the 1976 SRC-CPS National Election Study indicated that unemployed voters gave somewhat more support to Jimmy Carter than would be expected simply on the basis of their party loyalties. This does not, however, constitute unambiguous evidence of policy-oriented voting. As indicated earlier in this chapter (and as Schlozman and Verba explicitly recognized) jobless voters may have been supporting Carter because he was an unemployment-fighting Democrat, or they may also have been casting anti-incumbent votes against Ford. On the basis of evidence from this one election it is extremely difficult to determine whether or not (or in what proportions) voting was policy-oriented or incumbency-oriented.[35]

Fortunately, some better evidence on this hypothesis comes from Fiorina's study of retrospective voting.[36] Examining all presidential elections between 1956 and 1976, Fiorina assessed the impact of several variables, among them a dummy variable indicating whether or not the respondent's head of household had been out of work during the previous two years. In every election, regardless of the party of the president, voters whose head of household had been unemployed gave somewhat greater support to the Democratic candidate. To be sure, this analysis was largely exploratory in nature, and the equations differed substantially in form from his final voting model. Thus these findings, though encouraging, should be considered extremely tentative. Unfortunately, there is no comparable evidence for any type of election concerning the voting behavior of individuals who feel they have personally borne the brunt of inflation.

An Alternative to the Personal Experiences Hypothesis

Previous research, then, has generated some empirical support for the personal experiences hypothesis, although perhaps less than might have been expected given its intuitive and theoretical appeal. Voters' perceptions of recent trends in their families' financial situations do appear to lead to a modest amount of incumbency-oriented voting in presidential elections, but rarely exert a detectable impact upon their choices in other national elections. There is not much evidence one way or the other on this version of the policy-oriented hypothesis. What little there is, though, does suggest that voters respond in a policy-oriented manner to personally experienced unemployment.

On the whole, however, the performance of the personal experiences hypothesis has not been as impressive as that of an alternative proposition. According to this view, which will be referred to as the *national assessments* hypothesis, it is perceptions of national conditions and events which most heavily influence voting behavior. As before, the national assessments hypothesis can be applied to both incumbency-oriented and policy-oriented voting. In the first case, the prediction is that voters who believed the *nation's* economy was doing well would tend to support the incumbents, while those who believed it had worsened would tend to vote for the challengers. Similarly, such a version of the policy-oriented hypothesis posits that voters who see unemployment as a major national problem are more likely to support the Democrats, while those who believe the country is plagued by inflation turn instead to the Republicans. According to this hypothesis, then, economic problems, either in general or inflation and unemployment in particular, could well exert a strong influence over an individual's policy preferences and voting decisions without being personally troublesome.

It should be stressed that the distinction between these alternative hypotheses is not equivalent to the distinction between altruism and self-interest. True, it is difficult to believe that voters acting on the basis of personal economic experiences are motivated by something other than a self-interested concern for themselves and their families. Why voters might vote on the basis of national assessments, on the other hand, is less clear. Some may in fact be acting out of an altruistic or patriotic concern for the well-being of all Americans, or at least a large subset of them. On the other hand, voting on the basis of national assessments may be entirely motivated by self-interest: such voters may construe the performance or policies of the party in power as a public good, and thus use information about the condition of the nation's economy as an indicator of the present administration's ability to promote their own economic well-being—and incidentally that of their fellow citizens as well.

The difference between these two hypotheses is instead in the nature of the economic information they posit as having the greater influence upon voters' decisions. As has already been discussed, economic information gleaned from personal experience has the quality of being immediate, tangible, and of direct personal relevance. Information about conditions in the nations's economy, on the other hand, must be obtained from newspapers or television (or, to the extent that there is a two-step flow of communication, from other people's reports of items they have heard or seen in the news media). Informational differences of this nature are quite important, and our attention will return to this distinction fairly frequently. It must be kept in mind, however, that the difference between these two hypotheses is not in the degree of self-interestedness or public-regardingness that they ascribe to the American voter.

A potential problem with the national assessments hypothesis is in fact the greater attentiveness to public affairs it posits. A strong selling point of the personal experiences hypothesis, after all, is that it requires of the voter virtually no additional effort in securing political information. Available evidence, however, suggests that information costs are easily overestimated—or at least are not high enough to prevent most people from having some idea of what is going on in the country. In his examination of open-ended survey questions asking respondents to name what they felt were the most important problems facing the nation, Repass found that over 90% of all respondents in 1960 and 1964 could name at least one problem, and the average number mentioned was 2.5.[37] Furthermore, both Repass and Miller and Miller show that individuals' perceptions of important national problems faithfully reflect conditions and events in the real world. Miller and Miller's figures show that concern over the Vietnam War escalated right along with U.S. troop levels, then dropped off precipitously with the end of U.S. involvement in 1973. Racial problems topped the list in 1964, while concern over public order was frequently cited throughout the late sixties and early seventies. Similarly, public concern over economic issues, especially unemployment and inflation, rose as dramatically as the economy declined.[38]

Information costs, then, do not appear to present the national assessments hypothesis with any real difficulty. There are also some important theoretical points in its favor. Most arguments for this hypothesis usually begin with arguments against the personal experiences hypothesis. Kinder and Kiewiet contend that individuals largely attribute their own economic successes and failures to purely personal or local factors, e.g., getting a raise or a better job, making an unwise career choice, or trends in local business conditions.[39] Schlozman and Verba's survey evidence certainly backs them up. After examining the explanations of hundreds of unemployed people as to why they had lost their jobs, they report:

> What may be most significant is that the explanations of one's own loss of work tend to be narrow and contingent. Our respondents do not see themselves as victims of broad social forces or governmental ineptitude but of specific events connected with their particular employment circumstances.[40]

In other words, Americans generally believe that their own economic fortunes are largely determined by factors which have nothing to do with public policy or national economic trends. Thus personal economic experiences are rarely considered by voters when they make their decisions. The findings of a recent study by Feldman also support this argument. He found that when asked to explain why their family financial situation had worsened or improved in the previous year, only a small minority of respondents in the 1972 CPS survey referred to societal trends or to governmental policies. Those who did, however, showed a greater tendency to vote in an incumbency-oriented fashion in the 1972 presidential election than those who cited only personal, idiosyncratic factors.[41]

Sniderman and Brody make a related argument against the personal experiences hypothesis. In their view, it is Americans' enduring commitment to hardy individualism and the "ethic of self-reliance" which diffuses the political significance of personal economic problems. Data from the 1972 and 1974 National Election Studies strongly supported the claim that most people in this country believe that they themselves (not the government) are primarily responsible for solving or alleviating their own personal economic problems.[42] This argument should not be pushed too far, however. Schlozman and Verba found that few unemployed people go so far as to blame themselves, and most believe that they are entitled to assistance from the government in the form of unemployment compensation. But they too conclude that

> the prevailing theme is self-reliance. Most of our respond-
> ents do take for granted the accessibility of government
> assistance—as a matter of right, routine, or last resort.
> Very few, however, consider it as a means of avoiding their
> responsibility to take care of themselves. This, too, suggests
> that the political effects of the economic strain of jobless-
> ness would be contained.[43]

In contrast, according to proponents of the national assessments hypothesis, most people readily perceive trends in the
nation's economy to be a product of the policies pursued by those
in power.[44] An individual may attribute a personal loss of income
to unwise investments or to a cutback in overtime hours, but
believe a drop in GNP results from the ineptitude of the current
administration. A worker who has been laid off will blame it on
his or her company losing a contract to a competing firm, but see
a rise in the unemployment rate as the consequence of Republican macroeconomic policies. In short, trends in the nation's economy, in most people's minds, reflect directly upon the performance and policies of the governing party. Their own personal
economic fortunes, in contrast, generally do not.

There has been little analysis of public opinion data, unfortunately, to either bolster or challenge this argument. But as indicated earlier, the national assessments hypothesis has garnered an
impressive amount of support in several recent pieces of research,
and this line of reasoning would certainly help to account for it.
First, there is considerable evidence of national assessments
prompting incumbency-oriented voting. Analyses of data from
several CPS surveys show that voters who felt business conditions
in the country as a whole had worsened in the previous year were
less likely to support the incumbent president and congressional
candidates of his party than were voters who believed conditions
had improved.[45] Studies in this area also show a large measure of
incumbency-oriented voting in response to other national assessments, most notably ratings of the government's (presumably
taken to mean the incumbent administration) recent performance
in managing the economy. There is an explicitly political component in these ratings, which were, not surprisingly, highly correlated with more general partisan attitudes. But these and other
measures of perceived managerial competence continued to exert

a strong influence upon voting even when partisanship and overall ratings of the president were held constant.[46]

Second, on at least one occasion national economic assessments appear to have triggered a substantial amount of policy-oriented voting. Schlozman and Verba's analysis of data from the 1976 SRC-CPS election study indicated that individuals who felt unemployment was a more important problem for the nation cast considerably more votes for the Democratic nominee Carter than would have been expected on the basis of their expressed party identification. Those who felt inflation was the more pressing national problem, in contrast, provided Ford with a higher than expected percentage of their votes.[47] Tufte found the same thing in his examination of responses to a question on the 1976 NBC Election Day Poll which asked voters:

> In your opinion, which is the more important problem facing the country today: finding jobs for people who are unemployed, holding down inflation, or are both equally important?

As the national assessments version of the policy-oriented hypothesis would predict, voters who placed a higher priority on unemployment voted more Democratic, while those who were more concerned about inflation tended to prefer a Republican for president.[48] These data, unfortunately, come from only one election. Still the findings from these studies are impressive, in that there is no mistaking them for incumbency-oriented voting; the Republican recipient of votes from those who were more concerned about inflation, after all, was the incumbent president.

Summary

This chapter has delineated the two basic dimensions which underlie all the analyses to follow. First, is voting in response to economic concerns incumbency-oriented or is it policy-oriented? Several time series analyses have generated strong and pervasive support at the aggregate level for the incumbency-oriented hypothesis; a handful of others also found some evidence of policy-oriented voting, at least with regard to unemployment.

Second, do voters' decisions primarily reflect their own personal experiences with economic problems, or their assessments of economic conditions in the country as a whole? Several studies of the personal experiences version of the incumbency-oriented hypothesis have produced a rather mixed record of support: there appears to be a fair amount of evidence of such voting in presidential elections, but hardly any in other types of elections. As at the aggregate level, there has been little research on the policy-oriented alternative of this hypothesis, but the few scraps of evidence available do suggest that voters respond in a policy-oriented manner to personally encountered difficulties stemming from unemployment. Similarly, almost all examinations of the national assessments hypothesis have confined their attention to incumbency-oriented voting. These studies have afforded this hypothesis an impressive amount of empirical support. There is also some evidence of policy-oriented voting associated with perceptions of inflation and unemployment as serious national problems, but it comes only from the 1976 presidential election.

Previous research on the effects of economic concerns upon individual voting decisions has thus uncovered varying amounts of both incumbency-oriented and policy-oriented voting in response to both personal experiences and national assessments. The empirical record, however, is extremely fragmentary and thus inconclusive—this synopsis has been pieced together from scraps of evidence drawn from a collection of studies which never considered more than one of these two basic dimensions or pairs of alternatives. Moreover, all but a handful of these studies dealt with only one type of election, or with only one election year. And probably the worst deficiency in this area is that very few studies have brought any data to bear upon policy-oriented voting. In short, at this point it is simply impossible to assess the relative merits of the various hypotheses.

The present study, which will employ these two basic dimensions of analysis in examining voting in presidential and congressional elections between 1956 and 1980, will thus constitute a considerably more systematic study of the electoral effects of economic issues than has so far been conducted. It will, I hope, allow us to reach some firm conclusions about the empirical standing of the competing hypotheses. Before this task can be undertaken, however, there are some important methodological issues which must be addressed. This is the business taken up by the next chapter.

3
Estimating the Effects of Economic Concerns upon Voters' Decisions

Anyone taking a quick look at the public opinion/voting behavior literature will certainly be struck by the number of titles containing the word "confusion," "disarray," or "myth," or by the number of articles which claim to be revisions, reappraisals, or rejoinders. Many of the problems which give rise to this discouraging collection are inherent in the nature of the beast itself. Perceptions and attitudes are harder to measure than distance, area, or mass. Researchers do not work in a laboratory in which they can systematically control independent variables, but must work instead with whatever combination of conditions and events is present at the time data are collected. There is also the problem of causal inference—it is much harder to establish that a particular concern led voters to choose one candidate over another than, for example, that introduction of a catalyst produced an increase in the rate of a chemical reaction. Too often, however, voting studies simply launch into an analysis with only a superficial justification for proceeding as they do. All researchers in voting behavior must make hard and only partially satisfactory choices. Problems arise not so much in making these choices but in failing to be careful and explicit about them.

The aim of this or any other analysis of voting is to disentangle the independent effects of the variables of interest from those of a myriad of other variables which also enter into voters' decisions. The particular economic concerns being examined here, of course, are short-term factors, e.g., assessments of the course the nation's economy has taken during the previous year, or a recent spell of personally experienced joblessness. It is crucially important to distinguish between the effects of these factors and the effects of factors which exert a prior long-term influence upon voting behavior. The obvious strategy in this endeavor is to establish a stable, temporally prior baseline against which to measure changes induced by the particular short-term factors of interest.

With longitudinal or panel data, an excellent baseline is available, namely, the respondent's voting behavior in the previous election. The decisions of voters to either stand pat or to switch to different parties or candidates can then be traced to concerns, issues, and events which have intervened in the period between elections.[1] The effect of concerns over unemployment, inflation, or economic problems in general can thus be reliably differentiated from those of prior partisan attachments. Fortunately, the CPS National Election Study series contains two four-year panel studies—1956-60 and 1972-76. For the elections of 1958, 1960, 1974, and 1976, then, the following model (henceforth referred to as the Panel Model) will be estimated:

$$V^{p,c} = f(\beta_0 + \beta_1 R_{t-1}^{p,c} + \beta_2 D_{t-1}^{p,c} + \beta_k E_k + u)$$

where $V^{p,c}$ = respondent's reported vote for president or congressman, taking on the value of 0 if Democratic, 1 if Republican. Because of the dichotomous nature of the vote choice, this and all subsequent voting analysis will use probit analysis. (See appendix 1 for a discussion of this technique.)

   β_0 = a constant term.

   $R_{t-1}^{p,c}$ = a dummy variable, taking on the value of 1 if the respondent voted Republican in the previous election, 0 otherwise.[2]

   $D_{t-1}^{p,c}$ = a dummy variable taking on the value of 1 if the respondent voted Democratic in the previous election, 0 otherwise. A reference group is thus formed by those respondents who did not vote in the previous election.

E_k = one or more measures of concern over inflation, unemployment, or economic problems in general, at either a personal or national level.

u = a randomly distributed error term.

It is obviously impossible for any statistical model to specify all the variables which affect voters' decisions and yet retain any degree of parsimony. The Panel Model is no exception. The assumption we must live with, of course, is that the error term, which registers the cumulative effects of all unspecified variables, is randomly distributed; if not, estimates of the specified variables will be biased, at least partly the product of spurious correlation with the unspecified variables.[3] A potential manifestation of this problem in the Panel Model derives from the fact that voting in every election is influenced, to some degree, by factors which are idiosyncratic to that election. If the effects of these (unspecified) variables upon voting in the previous election are spuriously correlated with the effects of economic concerns upon voting in the current election, estimates of the latter will be biased. For example, blue-collar workers who simply could not stomach George McGovern in 1972 might also have suffered disproportionate amounts of unemployment in subsequent years. If so, their decisions to return to the Democratic fold in 1976, although mainly due to the absence of McGovern on the ticket, would wrongly appear to be the consequence of personally experienced unemployment.

In order to provide a check against this possibility, two variations on the Panel Model were constructed. The first simply substitutes the previous vote dummies with dummies registering the category of party identification (Democrat or Republican) expressed at that earlier time. The second alternative, based upon the approach taken by Jackson and Fiorina, utilizes a two-stage probit procedure.[4] In the first stage, party identification expressed at the time of the previous election is treated as a dependent variable with a larger battery of socioeconomic and demographic variables (completely exogenous to party identification) entered as independent variables. The predicted values of party identification are then entered as an "instrumental" variable into an equation which seeks to explain current vote choice.

Estimates generated by the Panel Model for the 1976 presidential election are displayed along with those produced by these two alternatives in table A.1 of appendix 3. As inspection of these figures indicates, the respective probit estimates generated by these models are extremely similar. It appears then, that results of the analyses of longitudinal data in this study are not much perturbed by varying the specifications of the Panel Model.

Cross-sectional Data

Unfortunately, the Panel Model can be used in only four of thirteen election years from 1956 to 1980. For the rest of the elections there is only data gathered in a single period. The strategy of analysis with cross-sectional data, however, is in principle the same as with longitudinal—to establish a stable, prior baseline against which to measure changes induced by various issue or candidate variables (in this case economic concerns). Following publication of Campbell and his associates' *The American Voter*, almost every study in voting behavior has pursued this strategy by adopting the concept of party identification.[5] Derived from reference group theory in social psychology, this view holds that voters have, with varying degrees of strength, long-term affective attachments to one of the two major parties. People's perceptions of themselves as Democrats or Republicans are largely the product of childhood socialization, preceding and thus powerfully influencing whatever opinions they come to hold about the major issues of the day. Party identification, by this line of reasoning, is thus of tremendous value in the analysis of cross-sectional data—although expressed contemporaneously with reported vote choice in a particular election, it exists prior to vote choice.

Furthermore, party identification has been seen to be an extremely *stable* attribute. Most importantly, it remains fixed while actual voting behavior changes from election to election; many voters will, on occasion, "defect" and vote for another party, but still retain their avowed party identification. It is much more stable over time than people's opinions on major political issues, and more stable than their ratings of prominent politicians.[6]

In its most refined form, party identification has been represented by a seven-point scale, ranging from "strong" Democrats, "weak" Democrats, Independents leaning Democratic, to "pure" Independents, Independents leaning Republican, "weak" Republicans, and "strong" Republicans. The scale thus contains both components of direction (Democrat, Independent, or Republican) and of strength (strong, weak, or leaning). By taking the expected turnout and vote direction percentages for the seven categories, a "normal vote" could be calculated, a vote based only upon long-term party loyalties with no other factors intervening.[7] Going a step further, the political impact of an issue could be registered with either an "L" (for long-term) statistic, i.e., the correlation between views on that issue and the party identification scale, or an "S" (for short-term) statistic—the effect of that issue on voting behavior after controlling for party identification.[8] Assuming partisanship to be fixed and temporarily antecedent to the voting decision, then, it could be specified as a baseline and precise estimates of the effects of concerns over inflation, unemployment, or economic problems in general could be obtained.

Unfortunately, a growing body of research clearly demonstrates that party identification does not fully possess the crucial properties which have been ascribed to it. First, party identification is not completely stable, and is downright unstable when the full seven-point scale is considered. Meier reports that only 38.3% of respondents in the CPS 1956-60 Panel Study remained at the same point on the scale throughout all three waves of the study. Even in the short run there was a great deal of instability: he found that only 60.1% of respondents in the Center for Opinion Research's September-November 1972 Panel were at the same point in both waves.[9] Available data indicate, however, that most of the instability takes the form of fluctuations in the strength of people's party attachments, and not in movements from one party category to another. Analyzing data from the 1956-58 and 1972-74 legs of the two CPS panel studies, Brody found that only about half the respondents in both panels retained the same strength of identification, but nearly 90% stayed in the same party category.[10]

This instability over time would not be a particularly bad problem if it were due primarily to randomly distributed measurement and categorization error. Unfortunately this is not the case. Brody found that movements in partisan strength were associated with individuals' candidate evaluations and issue positions.[11]. One of the main points of Fiorina's recent book is that partisanship is adjusted in response to retrospective evaluations of recent political and economic developments.[12] Rivers's analysis of CPS data led him to much the same conclusion.[13] And in a very complex system of simultaneous equations, Page and Jones found substantial amounts of simultaneity (reciprocal causation) between party identification, issue positions, and candidate evaluations.[14]

Finally, Shively found evidence of the worst sort of simultaneity.[15] Respondents who voted for a different party in 1958 than they had in 1956 were also more likely to change the direction of their party identification than those who did not vote for a different party. This means that in some cases considerations which led some voters to vote for a different party also prompted them to change their party identification. This is bad enough. But as Shively points out, other respondents—especially the party leaners—evidently took the questions pertaining to party identification to be questions about their current vote choice. Using party identification to predict the voting behavior of such respondents is, in a word, tautological.

In short, specification of the seven-point party identification scale in an equation estimating the effects of various economic concerns would not be a sound procedure. In all probability this measure of long-term partisanship would pick up some of the effects produced by these and other short-term forces. A far more reasonable estimation strategy would be to retain the basic concept of party identification, but to specify party categories only. Most of the instability which has been uncovered derives, after all, from fluctuations in the strength of partisan leanings, and not from movements across party categories. In the past few years a large number of researchers have employed this approach. A model of this nature can be stated as:

$$V^{p,c} = f(\beta_0 + \beta_1 R + \beta_2 D + \beta_k E_k + u)$$

where $V^{p,c}$ = respondent's reported vote for president or congressman, taking on the value of 0 if Democratic, 1 if Republican.

β_0 = a constant term.

R = a dummy variable, taking on the value of 1 if the respondent identifies with the Republican party (as either a strong or weak identifier, or as an Independent-leaning Republican), 0 otherwise.

D = a dummy variable taking on the value of 1 if the respondent identifies with the Democratic party (again, either strongly, weakly, or as a leaner), 0 otherwise. A reference group is thus formed by respondents who are "pure" Independents.

E_k = as before, one or more measures of concern over inflation, unemployment, or economic problems in general, at either the personal or national level.

u = a randomly distributed error term.

This model will henceforth be referred to as Cross-sectional Model 1. It will be estimated in the nine election years in the 1956-1980 series for which panel data are unavailable.

While this model is free of many of the problems which would result from employing the full seven-point scale, it is by no means completely satisfactory. Some respondents will have changed the direction of their party identification since the last election. A few others will still be reporting their current vote choice. And some simultaneity between party preference, vote decision, issue positions, and candidate evaluations may well still exist. Because of this, it is prudent to check estimates derived from Cross-sectional Model 1 with those from another model. This model, which will henceforth be referred to as Cross-sectional Model 2, dispenses entirely with party identification, and specifies instead a battery of socioeconomic and demographic variables as the baseline against which the effects of concerns over inflation and unemployment are gauged. These variables include educational attainment, occupation, family income, birth cohort, the region of the country in which one resides, race, union membership, and religion. (See appendix 2 for details on how this battery of social background variables was actually specified.) Cross-sectional Model 2, then, is as follows:

$$V^{p,c} = f(\beta_0 + \beta_j SB_j + \beta_k E_k + u)$$

where $V^{p,c}$ = respondent's reported vote for president or congressman, taking on the value of 0 if Democratic, 1 if Republican.

β_0 = a constant term.

SB_j = a battery of social background variables.

E_k = as before, one or more measures of concern over inflation and unemployment at either a personal or national level.

u = a randomly distributed error term.

This model avoids the problems which, to some extent, remain with Model 1's dummy variable specification. Above all, the social background variables it specifies are strictly exogenous to candidate evaluations, party preferences, and voting decisions. Although income, religion, race, and birth cohort are important determinants of political preferences, it is hard to believe that political preferences simultaneously affect one's income or religion, and even harder to believe that they affect one's race or birth cohort.

At the same time, Cross-sectional Model 2 has shortcomings of its own. First, the fixed background characteristics it specifies do not explain a great deal of the variance in voting behavior. Second, a very large percentage of voters do possess stable and enduring attitudes toward the major political parties. So although specifying an attitudinal variable such as party identification runs the risk of simultaneity bias and attenuated estimates of the effects of short-term economic concerns, *not* specifying a party identification variable may result in estimates which are biased upward.

What is important, though, is that while neither model is perfect, each tends to compensate for shortcomings in the other. In general, any bias in Model 2 should be upward, producing somewhat inflated estimates of the effects of economic concerns. The expected bias in Model 1, in contrast, will produce estimates which are somewhat attenuated. And to the extent the models produce estimates which are very close to each other, confidence in both models is greatly enhanced.

Still, as indicated earlier, in estimating the effect of various economic concerns upon voting it is highly desirable to have data which allow comparisons of voters' current decisions with the choices they made in the previous election. The Panel Model will thus be used in all elections for which the requisite data are available (1958, 1960, 1974, and 1976). In all other years the results tabulated in the main body of the text will be those derived from Cross-sectional Model 1, while those derived from Cross-sectional Model 2 will be reported in appendix 3. The discussion will take note of any important discrepancies in the two models' estimates.

The desired aim of both cross-sectional models, of course, is to produce estimates which are as similar as possible to those which would have been derived from the Panel Model had longitudinal data been present. All indications are that the models perform quite satisfactorily in this regard—the estimates they generate for the 1976 presidential election are very similar to those derived from the Panel Model and its variants (these results are also displayed in table A.1 of appendix 3). We can thus proceed with considerable assurance that in the analyses to follow estimates of the effects of economic concerns are not an artifact of the particular way in which the statistical models employed have been specified.

4
The Political Role of Personal Economic Experiences: A New Look at Some Old Evidence

The task to be undertaken in this chapter is to examine the personal experiences version of both the incumbency-oriented and policy-oriented hypothesis. As indicated in chapter 2, the vast majority of previous studies in this area looked mainly for evidence of incumbency-oriented voting in response to recent trends in voters' (and their families') financial conditions. These studies generally found a modest amount of support for the hypothesis in presidential elections, but whether or not voters believed they were financially better or worse off than a year ago rarely appeared to matter as far as their decisions in congressional, senatorial, or gubernatorial elections were concerned.

The survey researchers conducting these studies had hoped that the family finances item might point to individual level effects, which, when taken together, would account for the aggregate level connection between economic conditions and election outcomes. Thus these results, especially for congressional elections, were quite disappointing. The lack of supportive evidence, of course, could stem from problems with the measure rather than from shortcomings of the personal experience hypothesis. Responses to this question could reflect transient, superficial things, e.g., whether the weather is foul or fair, or if it is payday or the middle of a billing cycle, instead of a cold, hard assessment of one's economic fortunes over the course of the past year. This item, though, does seem to be a reasonably valid measure. Rosenstone and his associates found that answers to the family finances question were clearly a function of their objective status. Respondents who had a female head of household, were currently unemployed, or had low incomes were much more likely to report being worse off.[1] Similarly, the SRC Panel Study of Income Dynamics found that reports on family finances during the previous year accurately reflected actual changes in family income.[2]

Another objection often expressed against the family finances item is that responses to it are dominated by factors which are totally unrelated to either national economic trends or governmental economic policies. Local or regional movements in economic activity and life-cycle trends in earnings, investment, and consumption are often cited as such "extraneous" influences. This objection, however, is misplaced. The extent to which responses to this item are dominated by idiosyncratic factors has nothing to do with its validity—it merely seeks to ascertain whether respondents believe recent trends in their personal economic conditions have been favorable or unfavorable. This objection is, rather, an argument as to why ups and downs in people's economic fortunes—which is what the family finances item validly measures—would tend not to influence voting decisions. Indeed, it is the argument made against this hypothesis by Kinder and Kiewiet, an argument which, as indicated in chapter 2, Feldman's findings tended to support. Feldman found that only about a third of the voters in the 1972 CPS survey referred to societal or governmental factors as the reasons for changes in their familys' financial situation. This small subset of voters, though, exhibited a considerably stronger level of incumbency-oriented voting in response to these changes.[3] In short, this objection does not challenge the validity of the family finances measure, but it does challenge the personal experiences hypothesis itself.

In contrast to the large number of incumbency-oriented studies, there have been few examinations of the personal experiences version of the policy-oriented hypothesis. In fact, the studies which have the most direct bearing upon policy-oriented voting were actually looking for incumbency-oriented voting in response to unemployment. As before, there is some encouraging evidence from presidential elections: the results of Fiorina's exploratory analysis suggested that voters whose heads of household had been out of work gave greater support to Democratic candidates for president.[4] Similarly, Kinder and Kiewiet analyzed the behavior of such voters in congressional elections.[5] They found little evidence of incumbency-oriented voting, but did not consider the possibility that voting in response to personally encountered difficulties stemming from unemployment might be policy-oriented.

Probably the best way to begin the present examination of the personal experiences hypothesis is to take a new, more careful look at the family finances and head of household's unemployment measures, this time in light of both the incumbency-oriented and policy-oriented alternatives. As indicated earlier, Fiorina and Kinder and Kiewiet used the head of household unemployment measure to test for incumbency-oriented voting. It will be used here, however, to gauge the extent of policy-oriented voting. Both these previous studies specified the measure as a dummy variable, taking on the value of 1 if the head of household was either currently unemployed or had been unemployed sometime in the recent past. Although the length of this retrospective time frame varied somewhat from election study to election study, it often allowed episodes of joblessness which had occurred up to two years prior to the interview to be accounted. It would be hard to believe, however, that past experiences of unemployment are not discounted as time goes by.[6] This analysis will thus specify two dummy variables for unemployment instead of one. The first will take on the value of 1 if the respondent's head of household was currently unemployed, the second will do so if the family head was currently employed but had been out of work in the past. Furthermore, it just does not seem very likely that unemployment would retain much salience for a voter whose head of household had been out of work two years earlier but had been steadily employed since. The measure used in this analysis will therefore register only spells of unemployment which had occurred in the year prior to the election.

It should be remembered, however, that in using these measures to test the personal experiences version of the policy-oriented hypothesis, the following analysis must remain sensitive to the possibility that voting in response to unemployment may be incumbency-oriented. As suggested by the discussion in chapter 2, these two possibilities can be disentangled by comparing the effects registered by the unemployment dummies in elections in which the incumbent president was a Democrat with those in elections in which he was a Republican. Obviously, if voting is predominantly policy-oriented the effects will be consistently pro-Democratic, and if predominantly incumbency-oriented they will be consistently anti-incumbent. But if substantial amounts of both occur, the pattern will be a little more complicated. When the incumbent president is a Republican the two effects will coincide, but they will tend to cancel each other out when a Democrat is in office. As a result, estimates of the effects of personally encountered unemployment difficulties would be much larger in the former set of elections than the latter. The closer the size of these effects are in magnitude, the greater this asymmetry will be.

As for incumbency-oriented voting, this analysis can use the family finances measure in much the same manner as have previous studies. The actual specification of this measure will take the form of two dummy variables: one for voters who answered that they were better off financially than last year, another for voters who claimed to be worse off, with those who felt they were doing about the same forming the reference group. Besides being warranted on econometric grounds, this specification also allows testing a version of Bloom and Price's hypothesis that voting in response to economic conditions is incumbency-oriented, but asymmetric: voters punish incumbents for economic downturns, but do not reward them for improvements.[7] If so, feeling worse off financially should produce substantially stronger anti-incumbent effects than any pro-incumbent effects which result from feeling better off.

Just as it is necessary to remain sensitive to the possibility of incumbency-oriented voting in using the unemployment dummies to test the policy-oriented hypothesis, it is necessary to keep the possibility of policy-oriented voting in mind in using the family finances terms to test the incumbency-oriented hypothesis. This is because responses to the family finances question reflect a very wide range of economic experiences, including both inflation and unemployment. Some voters, for example, might report being worse off financially because of being laid off from work. Others might answer the question the same way, but because of difficulty in coping with rising food, fuel, or housing prices. While many voters may respond to these or other problems by voting in an incumbency-oriented manner, the response of others may be policy-oriented.

Indeed, the results of Weatherford's analysis of the 1958 and 1960 elections certainly suggest this possibility. His findings showed that (1) working-class voters were more likely than middle-class voters to report being financially worse off than they were a year or so earlier, and (2) that the relationship between these reported trends in personal financial fortunes and voting was much stronger for working-class voters than for middle-class voters.[8] The years 1958 and 1960, of course, were years of relatively low inflation and high unemployment. Many voters who reported being financially worse off were no doubt reporting unemployment-related problems, and they were concentrated in the working class. Weatherford's equations, though, did not specify any unemployment terms. What he may have been finding, then, was that among working-class voters incumbency-oriented voting was heavily supplemented by policy-oriented voting in response to unemployment, with both effects running in an anti-Republican direction.

On the unemployment side, of course, this problem has already been addressed. Voting in response to personally encountered unemployment, whatever the form it takes, would presumably be registered by the pair of unemployment dummies. There are, however, no indicators of personal economic difficulties stemming from inflation in this analysis. Incumbency-oriented voting prompted by a wide variety of economic variables, then, might be confounded with policy-oriented voting in response to inflation.

As before, these possible effects can be disentangled by comparing estimates of the family finances terms in elections in which the incumbent president was a Democrat with those in which he was a Republican. In inflationary years presided over by a Democrat, e.g., 1978 and 1980, policy-oriented voting favoring Republican candidates would coincide with incumbency-oriented voting, and estimates of the family finances "worse" term would be relatively large. In inflationary years in which the Republicans were in power, e.g., 1970 and 1974, policy-oriented and incumbency-oriented voting would run counter to each other, and as a result the estimates for the family finances "worse" term would be relatively small. And if there are no systematic differences between estimates in these two sets of years, it would indicate that the family finances terms are not picking up very much policy-oriented voting engendered by inflation.

There are a couple of additional points which should be addressed before proceeding. First, in a recent paper Kramer argues that if a cross-sectional analysis fails to control adequately for partisan predispositions, any residual covariance between these predispositions and changes in personal economic conditions could bias estimates associated with the family finances or similar measures. Moreover, depending upon the party of the incumbent president and the stage of the business cycle, the bias could run in either direction, suppressing estimates of incumbency-oriented voting in some years but inflating them in others.[9] These problems of estimation, according to Kramer, will result in an essentially random pattern of estimates with frequent sign reversals.

The probit equations to be employed in this analysis, of course, rely upon panel data wherever possible, and specify either party identification dummies or background socioeconomic variables when the only data available are cross-sectional. Still, this does not guarantee that none of this problematic covariance remains present. A way of assessing how serious this problem is, however, is to compare estimates from elections in which any expected bias due to this problem would run in opposite directions. In the time period under examination here, 1960 and 1980 are probably the best pair of elections available for this comparison. In 1960 the incumbent Republican administration presided over an economy sliding slowly into a recession. In 1980, on the other hand, the Federal Reserve's restrictive monetary policies led to record-high interest rates, a sharp drop in economic activity, and a jump in unemployment. In both cases, lower-income, working-class individuals—who tend to be more Democratic than the population as a whole—undoubtedly suffered disproportionately from the slowdowns. But because different parties were in power, any of the problematic covariance between partisan predispositions and trends in personal economic fortunes would tend to boost estimates of incumbency-oriented voting in 1960 but suppress the estimates in 1980.

A second methodological problem which needs to be taken into account arises from differences in the order in which questions were posed to respondents in the various National Election Studies. In a recent paper Sears and Lau assert that the observed association between the family financial situation measure and reported vote choice will be upwardly biased if the latter question is closely followed by the former on the survey.[10] Luckily, there were only two years in the series—1972 and 1976—in which this was the case. It is still wise, however, to be attentive to the possibility that estimates from these years will be inordinately large.

We are, at long last, ready to move on to the data. The results of this analysis of presidential and congressional election voting behavior from 1956 through 1980 are reported in tables 4.1 and 4.2, respectively. The last number in each entry is the probit estimate, the number in parentheses to the right the standard error. As indicated in chapter 3, estimates for the elections of 1958, 1960, 1974, and 1976 are derived from the Panel Model, while those for all other election years were generated by Cross-sectional Model 1. Democratic votes are coded 0 and Republican votes 1, so positive signs are pro-Republican in direction.

Probably the most striking feature of tables 4.1 and 4.2 is the consistently negative and thus pro-Democratic sign of the unemployment variables. In presidential elections eleven out of twelve are negative, as are nineteen out of twenty-four in the congressional election equations. Moreover, comparisons of the estimates in elections in which the incumbent president was a Democrat with those in which he was a Republican strongly indicate that the preponderance of voting in response to personal or familial encounters with unemployment was policy-oriented. There are no systematic differences at the congressional level between these two sets of elections, and the data on voting in presidential elections are also supportive of the policy-oriented hypothesis. True, by far the weakest estimates come from 1968, a year of Democratic incumbency, but the effects registered by the unemployment dummies in 1964 and 1980 were generally quite strong. This suggests that pro-Democratic, policy-oriented voting in 1968 may have been largely offset by the substantial inroads George Wallace made into the Democratic party's traditional blue-collar constituency. If this is what occurred it might arguably have been a form of incumbency-oriented voting. In general, though, voters from households whose breadwinner had been out of work gave more support to Democratic presidential and congressional candidates regardless of which party was in power at the time.

But while the pro-Democratic direction of this support is impressive in its consistency, it is often not impressive in magnitude. The strength of the probit estimates for the unemployment dummies varies widely. In the presidential election series, five

Table 4.1   The Effect of Head of Household's Unemployment and
Family Finances on Voting in Presidential Elections, 1956-1980

Variable	1956	1960	1964	1968[b]
Constant	.84/(.14)**	.01/(.08)	-.64/(.17)**	.56/(.17)**
Republican	.80/(.17)**	.58/(.09)**	1.28/(.18)**	1.04/(.19)**
Democrat	-1.53/(.14)**	-1.08/(.11)**	-.58/(.18)**	-1.24/(.17)**
Family finances better	.29/(.10)**	.15/(.09)*	-.05/(.10)	-.34/(.12)**
Family finances worse	-.24/(.12)*	-.02/(.11)	.14/(.14)	.17/(.15)
Head currently unemployed	***	-.71/(.30)**	-.99/(.71)	.04/(.46)
Head unemployed last year	—[a]	-.24/(.19)	-.55/(.32)*	-.03/(.35)
$\hat{R}^2$	.57	.33	.44	.55
n	1266	1149	1111	911

	1972	1976	1980[c]
Constant	.73/(.17)**	-.24/(.13)*	.66/(.17)**
Republican	.74/(.19)**	.77/(.13)**	.84/(.19)**
Democrat	-.83/(.17)**	-.73/(.15)**	-1.28/(.17)**
Family finances better	.03/(.12)	.13/(.10)	-.15/(.13)
Family finances worse	-.33/(.13)**	-.19/(.11)*	.14/(.13)
Head currently unemployed	-.20/(.27)	-.33/(.21)	-.85/(.31)**
Head unemployed last year	-.62/(.17)**	-.13/(.16)	-.10/(.17)
$\hat{R}^2$	.39	.32	.51
n	827	923	877

a. The 1956 study did not ask respondents about any past unemployment suffered
by their family head. b. Wallace voters were excluded from the analysis in 1968.
c. Anderson voters were excluded from the analysis in 1980.
* $p < .05$ ** $p < .01$ ***Not included in equation because of very low n.

Table 4.2   The Effect of Head of Household's Unemployment and
Family Finances on Voting in Congressional Elections, 1956-1980

Variable	1956	1958	1960	1962
Constant	.15/(.13)	-.36/(.11)**	-.15/(.09)*	-.33/(.21)
Republican	1.02/(.15)**	1.01/(.12)**	1.27/(.12)**	1.42/(.22)**
Democrat	-1.51/(.14)**	-.95/(.13)**	-.76/(.10)**	-.90/(.21)**
Family finances better	.28/(.11)**	.20/(.11)*	.03/(.10)	-.05/(.14)
Family finances worse	-.02/(.14)	-.19/(.15)	-.05/(.13)	.12/(.17)
Head currently unemployed	***	-.49/(.40)	-.61/(.37)*	-.30/(.49)
Head unemployed last year	—^{a}	-.42/(.24)*	.02/(.23)	-.21/(.26)
$\hat{R}^2$	.60	.44	.42	.56
n	1157	825	987	697

	1964	1966	1968
Constant	-.60/(.20)**	.02/(.17)	-.11/(.16)
Republican	1.27/(.20)**	1.02/(.19)**	1.02/(.18)**
Democrat	-.63/(.20)**	-.83/(.18)**	-.71/(.17)**
Family finances better	.09/(.10)	-.12/(.13)	.10/(.11)
Family finances worse	.08/(.16)	-.48/(.14)**	.31/(.14)*
Head currently unemployed	-.39/(.56)	-.65/(.57)	-.65/(.54)
Head unemployed last year	.23/(.26)	—^{a}	-.23/(.36)
$\hat{R}^2$	.44	.43	.41
n	957	677	871

* $p < .05$ ** $p < .01$ ***Not included in equation because of very low n.

Table 4.2   The Effect of Head of Household's Unemployment and
Family Finances on Voting in Congressional Elections   *(cont.)*

Variable	1970	1972	1974
Constant	-.07/(.16)	-.25/(.17)	-.54/(.13)**
Republican	1.06/(.19)**	1.03/(.19)**	1.13/(.13)**
Democrat	-.83/(.18)**	-.70/(.19)**	-.55/(.13)**
Family finances better	.02/(.19)	.04/(.13)	.04/(.13)
Family finances worse	-.03/(.19)	.04/(.15)	.16/(.27)
Head currently unemployed	-.51/(.48)	-.44/(.34)	-.16/(.27)
Head unemployed last year	-.29/(.37)	-.39/(.21)*	-.01(.18)
$\hat{R}^2$	.45	.41	.36
n	683	692	863

	1976	1978	1980
Constant	-.49/(.12)**	-.05/(.14)	-.14/(.16)
Republican	1.20/(.14)**	.69/(.14)**	.76/(.16)**
Democrat	-.21/(.12)*	-.60/(.14)**	-.57/(.16)**
Family finances better	.35/(.12)**	-.16/(.11)	-.09/(.12)
Family finances worse	-.18/(.13)	-.18/(.11)*	.05/(.12)
Head currently unemployed	.17/(.12)	-.24/(.32)	-.11/(.29)
Head unemployed last year	-.19/(.20)	-.05/(.14)	.18/(.16)
$\hat{R}^2$	.31	.27	.29
n	689	1009	859

a. The 1956 and 1966 studies did not ask respondents about any past unemployment suffered by their family head.
* $p < .05$ ** $p < .01$ ***Not included in equation because of very low n.

estimates exceed .5, but three are .1 or less; in congressional elections only four are greater than .5, but five fall under .1. The difference between effects of these sizes is substantial. If there is a 50% chance that a certain voter will vote Democratic, an estimate of .5 would, everything else held constant, increase his probability of voting Democratic to 69.2%; an estimate of .1 would move it up to only 54.1%. Another indication of how weak the estimates often are is that most do not attain conventional levels of statistical significance. To be sure, the number of voters in the unemployment categories was often very small: in the congressional election series up through 1970, an average of only twenty-seven voters reported that their family head had been unemployed during the previous year, and only thirteen on average indicated that he or she was currently out of work (the smallest number, in 1966, was nine). The large standard errors resulting from the small size of these categories make statistical significance difficult to achieve. The average level of unemployment in the 1970s, however, was a good deal higher than it had been in the previous decade, and the number of voters in the two categories was much larger. In the congressional elections from 1972 through 1980 the average number of voters whose family head was either currently unemployed or had been so in the previous year rose to twenty-seven and seventy, respectively. Low *n* is thus much less of a problem here. So although voters from families which had been affected by unemployment appeared to give greater support to Democratic candidates in this series of elections, the magnitude of this support was often of very modest proportions.[11]

Much of the variation in the electoral impact of personal or familial unemployment, however, is systematic. First, such experiences generally exerted a greater influence upon voting in presidential elections than in congressional. As indicated earlier, the proportion of estimates exceeding .5 is much higher in the former set of elections, as is the proportion of estimates which are statistically significant. And a direct comparison of the unemployment terms in congressional and presidential elections occurring on the same date shows that estimates in presidential elections are larger (i.e., more pro-Democratic) in eight of twelve cases. This is to be expected. Congressional races are of much less interest to most citizens than are contests for the presidency, and so the impact of issue concerns upon their voting decisions is weaker. Interestingly, though, estimates of the unemployment dummies appear to be pretty strong in the first several congressional elections, and then fall off toward the end of the series. None of them from 1974 on are very large, and a couple are pro-Republican in direction. Moreover, this decline predates the return of the Democrats to power after 1976, and thus would not seem to result from a confounding of incumbency-oriented and policy-oriented voting.

Second, it also appears that voters' decisions reflect a discounting of past bouts of unemployment. In fifteen of the eighteen equations reported in tables 4.1 and 4.2 in which comparisons can be made, voters whose family head was currently unemployed gave more support to Democratic candidates than did voters whose family head was currently working but had been unemployed in the previous year. Another strong indication that episodes of familial unemployment do not remain salient for very long is provided by the data in table 4.3, which cross-tabulates the recent employment history of respondent's heads of household with their responses to the family finances question. As this table

Table 4.3   Trends in Family Financial Situation and Head of Household's Recent Employment History, 1980

Head of household's previous year employment history	Family financial situation compared to last year			
	Better	Same	Worse	*n*
Never unemployed	33.5	26.5	40.0	1375
Was unemployed but currently working	32.2	20.5	47.3	146
Currently unemployed	12.5	13.9	73.6	72
All respondents	32.4	25.4	42.2	1593

shows, nearly three-fourths of the respondents whose head of household was currently unemployed reported that their family's financial condition had worsened in the past year. In contrast, responses to the family finances question given by those whose head of household had been out of work but was currently employed were, overall, barely distinguishable from reports given by those whose head of household had never been unemployed in the previous twelve months. (The data reported in table 4.3 are taken from the 1980 National Election Study, but results of this analysis performed upon data from several other years were very similar.) Once a spell of joblessness has ended, then, the salience of that experience and its impact upon voting appear to recede quickly.

Discounting past episodes of joblessness would obviously tend to limit the cumulative electoral effect of personally experienced unemployment. In arguing *for* the political potency of unemployment, Arthur Okun frequently pointed out that although only a small percentage of people are jobless at any one time (usually), many times that number have been out of work sometime during the previous year.[12] This fact is reflected, of course, in the relative sizes of the two unemployment categories in this series of election surveys. If, however, the potential effects of personally encountered unemployment upon voting decisions are dissipated as rapidly as these figures suggest, such difficulties would necessarily have only a very small impact on election outcomes.

A number of aggregate level studies on the electoral effects of economic conditions have also concluded that the electorate has a short memory. Although there were not enough data points to derive very precise estimates, Fair's analysis found that economic conditions in the second and third quarters of the election year best predicted votes for president.[13] Similarly, Kernell found that inflation and unemployment best predicted presidential popularity when change in their levels across the previous six months was considered.[14] At least as far as personal experiences with unemployment are concerned, then, this study's findings about individual voters accord nicely with these findings about the electorate as a whole.

The other economic indicators included in the equations displayed in tables 4.1 and 4.2—the family finances "better" and "worse" dummies—performed very much as they had in previous studies. The signs of all fourteen terms in the seven presidential elections were in accord with the incumbency-oriented hypothesis; compared to voters who felt their financial situation had stayed the same during the previous year, those who felt they were better off gave greater support to the incumbent, and those who felt worse off gave him less. In five of the elections at least one of the terms was statistically significant, and in 1980, even though neither term was significantly different from the reference group in the middle, the difference between the "better" and "worse" terms was statistically significant ($p<.05$). With sample sizes as large as the ones in table 4.1, of course, statistically significant estimates may often be quite small and substantively unimportant. The effects registered here, though, are not trivial. Given that the average difference between the pair was .34, feeling that one's financial situation had improved recently instead of worsened could, *ceteris paribus*, increase a voter's probability of opting for the incumbent by as much as 13%.

It should also be noted that estimates in 1960 do not appear to be unusually large, nor do the estimates in 1980 appear to be especially small. It appears, then, that estimates of the family finances terms were not perturbed by spurious, unmeasured correlation with voters' partisanship, and thus were not compromised by the estimation problems described by Kramer. Indeed, these measures generate clear evidence of incumbency-oriented voting in good years and in bad, with Republicans in the White House as well as Democrats. It is also the case that the estimates from 1972 and 1976 were not relatively larger (or smaller) than estimates from other years. Differences between estimates of the "better" and "worse" terms were .36 and .32, respectively, compared to the series average of .34. Thus the proximity of the family finances and vote report questions in these two election studies apparently did not induce a stronger observed association.[15]

The figures reported in table 4.1, finally, tend not to support this particular version of the asymmetric incumbency-oriented hypothesis. Averaging estimates across the seven presidential elections, the mean of the probit estimates associated with the family finances "better" term was .162, compared to .175 for the "worse" terms. In this series of elections, then, incumbent presidential candidates were rewarded by voters who felt their economic circumstances had improved in about the same measure as they were punished by those who felt worse off economically.

Moving on to table 4.2, it is obvious that support for the personal experiences version of the incumbency-oriented hypothesis, as was the case in previous studies, is much harder to come by at the congressional level. Although the signs of a large majority of estimates are consistent with incumbency-oriented voting, they are rarely very large. Looking across the entire series of congressional elections from 1956 through 1980, the average of the differences between the "better" and "worse" terms was only .1. An effect of this size could move the probability of voting for or against the incumbent by a maximum of 4%. As a consequence very few of the family finances terms are statistically significant, and two that are (in 1966 and 1978) are in the wrong direction.

In an earlier discussion the worry was expressed that in some years policy-oriented voting in response to inflation might be mixed in with incumbency-oriented voting in response to economic difficulties of all kinds. This worry appears to have been unfounded. To be sure, the estimate of the family finances "worse" term in 1970 was quite small (suggesting anti-Republican incumbency-oriented voting and pro-Republican policy-oriented voting in response to inflation tended to cancel each other out) and it was in a pro-Republican direction in 1974 (suggesting that policy-oriented voting tended to dominate incumbency-oriented voting). But estimates of this term in 1978 and 1980, inflationary years presided over by the Democrats, hardly indicate the presence of incumbency-oriented and policy-oriented voting acting in concert. Both estimates in 1980 are quite small, albeit in the correct direction. The pattern was quite muddled in 1978—estimates of the "better" and "worse" terms were nearly identical, and the negative, pro-Democrat sign of the statistically significant "worse" term runs counter to the prediction of both hypotheses.

In discussing the impact of personally encountered unemployment upon voting in congressional elections, it was noted that estimates of the unemployment dummies were fairly large early in the series but tailed off toward the end. The pattern of estimates of the family finances terms over time is considerably fuzzier, but there is some suggestion of this same trend. Things start out well, with the 1956 and 1958 equations each containing a statistically significant estimate. But after 1970 estimates are usually under .1, and if greater than that are as likely to be in the wrong direction as not. Again, the evidence for this trend is quite weak, and it would be unwise to stake very much on whether it is there or not. However, there is no mistaking the steady drop in the explanatory power of the entire equation across this series of elections. $\hat{R}^2$s dropped from .60 in 1956 to less than half that in 1978 and 1980.[16] The apparent erosion in the influence of personal economic experiences upon voting in congressional elections, then, would seem to have occurred contemporaneously with a decline in the influence of other, more important factors—most notably the voters' partisan loyalties. The $\hat{R}^2$s in table 4.1, in contrast, do not reveal a similar drop in the predictive power of the equations in presidential elections.

All in all, then, the findings in table 4.2 are quite consistent with those of previous studies—whether voters believed their own financial situation was improving or worsening rarely had much effect upon the amount of support they gave to congressional candidates of the incumbent president's party. As most of these studies have concluded, it is doubtful that the aggregate impact of this variable could account for the strong aggregate level connection between economic conditions and congressional elections.[17]

Summary

By now the head of household's unemployment and family finances measures have probably been pushed as far as (if not farther than) is warranted. As for the personal experiences version of the incumbency-oriented hypothesis, the results of the present analysis have corroborated those of previous studies. In most presidential elections, voters who believed their family's financial situation had improved during the previous year were more likely to support the incumbent president than were voters who believed their family's financial situation had worsened. There was far less support for this hypothesis, however, at the congressional level. Comparison of the estimates of the two family finances terms in each congressional election equation did not indicate that feeling worse off financially exerted a greater influence upon voters' decisions than feeling better off.

In its analysis of the personal experiences version of the policy-oriented hypothesis, though, the present study has gone considerably beyond previous efforts. Results here indicate that voters whose head of household was unemployed gave greater support to Democratic presidential and congressional candidates in virtually every election examined. This effect, however, was considerably weaker among voters whose family head had been unemployed in the previous year but was currently working. This and other evidence indicated that people tend to discount past experiences with unemployment fairly quickly.

Finally, the policy-oriented effects of the head of household unemployment variable and incumbency-oriented effects of the family finances measure appeared to have been stronger in the beginning of the congressional elections series than at the end. Moreover, this decline in the size of the estimates of these variables was paralleled by a substantial drop in the overall explanatory power of the entire congressional election equation.

There remain, obviously, some important shortcomings in this analysis. The unemployment measures, for instance, are objective ones; it would be very useful to have indicators of the subjective salience of unemployment and its resultant difficulties. Most importantly, this analysis generated no direct evidence on the effects of personal difficulties with inflation. What is needed to continue this line of inquiry, then, are new measures, richer in information about the specific economic problems which people confront. The task of developing and analyzing such new measures is undertaken in the next chapter.

5
Policy-oriented Voting in Response to Self-defined Personal Economic Problems

What is needed in order to conduct a more compelling test of the personal experiences version of the policy-oriented hypothesis is a means of isolating groups of voters who find various economic problems—inflation and unemployment in particular—salient and troublesome. The analysis in the previous chapter included no specific indicator of personally experienced difficulties with inflation, and its measures of unemployment simply indicated whether the respondent's head of household was currently or had recently been out of work. Although such a measure is reasonably valid, a subjective indicator of unemployment and unemployment-related difficulties would permit some desirable refinements. As indicated earlier, many single heads of household were young workers, and it is likely that at least some of them were not all that interested in stable careers. For them, periodic or seasonal layoffs—especially when they provide eligibility for compensation—are not necessarily an unattractive feature of a job.[1] Conversely, many workers who are currently employed may not be able to work as many hours as they would like, or may be worried about losing their job in the near future. Being unemployed is thus neither a necessary nor sufficient condition for viewing unemployment as a pressing personal problem.

In the analysis to follow, then, individuals who did perceive unemployment, inflation, or other economic problems to be personally troublesome are identified by their responses to a battery of open-ended questions included in all three legs of the 1972-76 CPS American Panel Study. Respondents were asked:

> Let's change the subject for a moment. We like to have people tell us what sorts of problems they have to deal with in their daily lives. Can you tell me what some of the problems are that you face these days in your life? . . . Anything else?

Their answers to these questions were used to construct indicators of self-defined, personal economic problems. Unfortunately, the machine-readable coding categories developed by the CPS for these items were, for present purposes, not appropriate. One of the major problems with the 1976 coding scheme was that complaints about unemployment were lumped together with all other job-related references, which ranged from despising the boss to having to work too many hours. Indeed, only about half of the references in the employment-related category were about unemployment. The 1972-74 codes often contained a wide variety of responses. One category, for example, contained references to inflation, taxes, governmental waste, and the cost of college. These responses obviously needed to be disaggregated. It was therefore necessary to recode responses as they appeared on the original protocols.[2] Initial apprehension that respondents would resist these probes into their personal lives proved unwarranted. Rather, most seemed to warm to the task, welcoming the opportunity to unburden themselves. The hundreds of different problems they cited, ranging from being swamped by too many installment payments to waxy yellow buildup on the kitchen floor, provided a rich mosaic of American life in the seventies.

Another fear—that they would be reticent about mentioning economic problems—also proved groundless. Well over half the respondents referred to at least one economic problem. The 1972-76 period was not, after all, the most prosperous of times. The key problem in this entire analysis, then, was to collapse the myriad responses into a manageable number of categories. References to unemployment and inflation were naturally sorted out, but categories of other important economic problems could be derived from the verbatim interview data as well. The coding scheme which was thus developed, along with the marginal frequencies from all three years, is presented in table 5.1. What are reported are the respondents' most important personal *economic* problems. If a respondent mentioned some noneconomic problem as the most important one he or she faced, e.g., poor health, but also mentioned an economic problem, the economic problem was the one which was coded here.[3]

Table 5.1   Most Important Personal Economic Problems (*percentages*)

Problem reported	*1972*	*1974*	*1976*
Inflation	14.4	30.2	22.2
Declining real income	4.8	7.1	5.9
Unemployment related	3.4	4.4	4.0
Taxes	5.5	1.3	4.1
General economic problems	18.6	19.2	19.8
Noneconomic problems	32.5	24.4	26.8
No problem mentioned	20.8	13.4	17.2
Total	100.0	100.0	100.0
n[a]	1109	2523	2415

a. ns are based on the 1972, 1974, and 1976 cross-sectional weighted samples of all respondents. No major turnout effects were present, however, so the percentages reported here are virtually identical when voters only are considered. Weights are *not* used in any of the probit analyses.

As table 5.1 shows, respondents cited *inflation* more frequently than any other economic problem. This category includes all references to high or rising prices, either for specific commodities like food or fuel oil, or prices in general. As many economists have suspected, few people differentiated between high prices and rising prices. Respondents used the terms interchangeably: complaints such as "high food prices—inflation in general" and "the high cost of living—rising heating costs" were quite common.

And the distinction may be little more than a difference in temporal perspective, i.e., prices are high now because of past inflation but rising because of continuing inflation. Confidence that this category registers what it is supposed to is bolstered by the fact that the percentage of respondents naming inflation their worst personal economic problem corresponded closely to the objective rate of inflation which obtained in these years (the Consumer Price Index rose by 3.3% in 1972, 11.0% in 1974, and 5.8% in 1976).

Many economists have suspected that there is substantial confusion among the public concerning inflation and its costs. After all, it is *real* incomes and *real* prices which should concern people, not the nominal price level. Thus widespread public aversion to inflation, they have argued, results mainly from people confusing inflation with a declining real income. Such confusion is understandable—the typical way real incomes are reduced is for price inflation to outpace wage increases. People may thus blame the mechanism (price inflation) instead of the end result (a lower real income).

But as table 5.1 indicates, between 5 and 7% of the respondents in these surveys did refer explicitly to a *declining real income*. A variety of responses were subsumed under this category: failure of wages to keep up with price increases; living on a fixed income and being squeezed by inflation; complaints about declining purchasing power ("I've got more dollars but they don't go as far"). This category also includes complaints about failing to maintain the standard of living one is accustomed to, or having great difficulty in doing so, e.g., being forced to work extra hours or taking a second job in order to pay the bills.

Given that there is undoubtedly some confusion in many people's minds between inflation per se and real income losses, one might question the wisdom of differentiating between these respondents and those in the inflation category. It makes sense to do so, however, on two grounds. First, it is very possible that respondents in the declining real income category were suffering (or believed they were suffering) more economic hardship than those who simply cited inflation. Second, individuals who referred to a declining real income may have been more sophisticated in perceiving the true nature of their problems.

The *unemployment related* category is broadly defined. It contains all respondents who felt their worst economic problem was that they (or persons close to them) were laid off, unemployed, worried by the threat of unemployment, or underemployed, i.e., unable to work enough hours. Despite the breadth of this definition, surprisingly few respondents fell into this category—between 3.4 and 4.4%. It might be argued that many respondents felt references to unemployment would reflect badly on themselves, and thus chose to name some other problem. This seems very unlikely, however, given that they showed no reluctance to admit that they (or family members) were out of work in response to other questions. No doubt a major reason why this category is so small is the fact that unemployment compensation and other programs have taken some of the sting out of joblessness. On the other hand, unemployment is surely no bed of roses for workers and their families: although about 80% of the labor force is covered by some form of unemployment insurance, such compensation generally falls far short of making up for lost income. As Cameron points out, the unemployed come disproportionately from that segment of the labor force which is not covered by compensation programs, and benefits for those who are covered amount, on average, to less than half the gross earnings of the typical production worker.[4] But in any case, the figures in table 5.1 indicate that the percentage of respondents naming unemployment their worst problem was lower than the objective rate of unemployment.

Similarly, not too many respondents referred to *taxes* as their worst personal economic problem. The percentage was higher in the relatively prosperous year of 1972 (5.5%) and lower in the recession year of 1974 (only 1.3%). Perhaps there is a sort of rough hierarchy in the perception of economic problems, with taxes becoming salient only when other problems—e.g., unemployment, rising prices—appear to pose no immediate danger. While there are any number of taxes one might find distasteful, in most cases it could not be ascertained what form of taxation the respondent was alluding to. A residual category, *general or miscellaneous economic problems*, was largely composed of vague references to such things as "bills," "money problems," or "not making enough money." As table 5.1 shows, the percentage of respondents falling into this category was remarkably stable from year to year—around 20% each time. In fact, the size of most categories remained quite stable from year to year; only the percentage citing inflation fluctuated much. And as indicated earlier, the size of the inflation category clearly reflected the actual rates of inflation in 1972, 1974, and 1976.

The labels of the two remaining categories are self-explanatory. People who reported literally hundreds of different types of problems ended up in the *noneconomic problems* category. Most of these were ordinary, day-to-day problems, such as obnoxious neighbors, inattentive spouses, or poor health. None of the problems they mentioned in response to the initial survey question or follow-ups, however, had any economic content whatsoever. Respondents in the last category, finally, simply did not report any problems at all.

Cross-tabular analyses of the reported economic problems revealed several important differences between personally encountered inflation and unemployment problems, as well as differences between them and some of the other problems which were coded. First of all, as is shown in table 5.2, those individuals who cited unemployment in 1976 were much more likely than average to report that their (family's) financial situation had worsened during the previous year. Table 4.3 in the previous chapter, similarly, demonstrated that respondents whose head of household was currently out of work were also considerably more likely than average to report being worse off financially. This is probably about what we should expect, given the serious objective economic costs of unemployment.

Respondents in the inflation category, on the other hand, appeared to differ little in their assessments of their family financial conditions. Thirty-three percent of them reported being financially worse off than a year ago, a figure barely distinguishable from the total sample rate of 30%. These data suggest that a large share of the discomfort associated with inflation is *not* attributable to objective economic losses. Hibbs is almost certainly right, therefore, in concluding that "less tangible subjective and psychological factors are more important than objective costs in explaining widespread public aversion to inflation."[5] Surely one such factor, as hinted earlier, is the failure of many people to make the connection between rising prices and rising wages. As shown in Katona's study, they tend to consider increases in their income the well-deserved result of their own efforts—doing a good job, acquiring more skill and experience, getting a promotion or better job, etc. Only a small minority of respondents in his surveys reported that their income had risen on account of better business

Table 5.2 Family Financial Situation by Most Important
Personal Economic Problems, 1976

Most important personal economic problems	Family financial situation compared to a year ago			
	Better	Same	Worse	*n*
Inflation	30.0	36.6	33.3	423
Declining real income	24.6	26.3	49.1	114
Unemployment related	28.9	26.3	44.7	76
Taxes	37.8	27.0	35.1	74
General economic problems	35.0	30.2	34.7	331
Noneconomic problems	37.4	38.7	23.9	556
No problem mentioned	37.8	44.3	18.0	323
Total	34.3	36.0	29.7	1897

conditions, union efforts, or from inflation-induced COLA increases.[6] So although most people are evidently not using inflation as a code word for real income losses, they probably do see it as something which prevents their purchasing power from going up as much as it should have.

There is another important "psychological" factor which accounts further for aversion to inflation. It is, however, a true cost, in no way resulting from a perceptual bias. Inflation increases the information costs entailed in everyday economic decision-making. Because of it, the past price of a certain good becomes a less valid indicator of what a reasonable price for the same good should be at present. People thus feel greater uncertainty about whether or not they are spending their money wisely, or whether their wages are suitable reward for the work they do. And as Katona and Okun have both noted, stable prices are imbued with notions of fairness: when prices instead are rising, people become more anxious as to whether they are paying a "fair" price for a good or service or are being ripped off.[7]

Finally, the figures in table 5.2 confirm the wisdom of distinguishing between respondents who reported a declining real income as their most serious personal economic problem from those who simply cited inflation. Individuals in the former category, unlike those in the latter, were far more likely to feel that their family's financial situation had worsened. Indeed, their assessments were even more negative than those of respondents in the unemployment category.[8]

In short, these findings are consistent with the findings of previous research. Unemployment often results in serious economic hardship. The major immediate costs inflation inflicts upon individuals, however, appear to be the less tangible though nonetheless real costs of living in a less predictable and thus anxiety-provoking world.

Results of further analyses of these problem reports, similarly, were quite in keeping with another central finding of previous research: inflation and unemployment differ in the way their costs are distributed. The percentages of respondents citing unemployment and related difficulties, first of all, closely paralleled the objective rates of joblessness prevailing among different racial and occupational groups. According to the 1976 cross-sectional data, blacks were more than twice as likely as whites to refer to unemployment—7.9% compared to 3.7%. Among occupational categories the percentages ranged from only 1.6% of managerial-administrative personnel to 14.0% of nonfarm laborers. Reports that one's most serious personal economic problem was a declining real income were also associated with objective demographic and economic characteristics. In particular, retirees and individuals with low incomes were considerably more likely than average to fall into this category.

In contrast, there was little correlation between respondents' propensity to cite inflation and a host of background socioeconomic characteristics. The relationship with family income, for example, is tenuous at best. In the 1976 cross-sectional sample, the percentage citing inflation was lowest in the lowest income category—13.6%. In the other categories, though, the percentage varied erratically between 20 and 29%.[9] (Income was measured by a nine-point ordinal scale.) Housewives, who presumably do disproportionate amounts of the household shopping, were also somewhat more likely to name inflation their worst economic problem. When other background characteristics, e.g., age, sex, race, or union membership, were considered, no reliable differences could be detected at all.

These findings imply (to the extent subjective perceptions mirror objective conditions) that inflation tends not to help or harm members of different demographic or socioeconomic groups systematically. At first this would seem to run counter to the economics literature reviewed by Hibbs, which indicates, in his words, that "lower income and occupational groups are best served by a relatively low unemployment—high inflation macroeconomic configuration."[10] Furthermore, it would appear to run counter to survey data which Hibbs cites. He found that when asked "which of the two problems—inflation or unemployment—do you think will cause the more serious economic hardship for people during the next year or so?," respondents from lower-status, blue-collar occupations were more likely to name unemployment (and less likely to name inflation) than their higher-status, white-collar counterparts.[11]

The contradiction, however, is more apparent than real. For this is exactly the pattern which would emerge if these groups were, as indicated by the present analysis, roughly equal in their aversion to inflation but differentially averse to unemployment.[12] A closer reading of Hibbs's discussion of the objective costs of inflation and unemployment, moreover, makes clear the fact that lower income and occupational groups do not benefit from inflation per se. Rather, it is that when labor markets are tight, such workers suffer lower rates of unemployment and earn relatively higher wages. Although this situation tends to be inflationary, it is the demand for their labor, not inflation, which benefits these workers.

This reading of Hibbs's discussion, furthermore, is backed up by the findings of several econometric studies. Although each of these studies finds some evidence of inflation redistributing income and wealth, these effects are quite small and very complicated (e.g., a tiny shift of relative income shares from the top and bottom quintiles to the middle three). Probably the most important of these is a masterful piece of work by Piachaud.[13] In agreement with most economists, Piachaud assumes that perfectly anticipated inflation would result only in a change in the numbers registering the relative value of goods and services.[14] And it is by definition true that unanticipated inflation benefits net debtors and harms net creditors when assets and liabilities are in fixed prices. But as Piachaud's analysis of postwar Britain demonstrates, for the most part these effects cancel each other out. The largest holders of fixed-rate financial assets, i.e., the rich, are thereby hurt by inflation; but these same people are usually the largest holders of real estate and other physical assets, which usually appreciate in value more quickly during periods of rapid inflation. High rates of inflation also mean higher interest rates for home mortgage holders, but this is generally outweighed by the fall in the real value of their debt. Inflation-generated "bracket creep" tends to make income tax schedules more progressive, but it also places the threshold at which people begin to pay taxes much lower in the income distribution. Although fixed income occupational pensions have certainly declined in value, social security benefits, which have been indexed since 1974 in the United States, have been boosted fairly frequently. And as Piachaud points out, the dynamic effects of inflation are even more complicated. People are often hurt by inflation, but for any one of several reasons may benefit from it a few years later.

Finally, it is often argued that the price of food, fuel, and other necessities generally inflates at a higher rate than do nonessential goods; if true, lower-income groups, who spend a higher percentage of their income on necessities, would be disproportionately hurt. Vasilatos and Hibbs calculated occupation- and age-specific price indices (based upon the average "basket" of goods and services typically purchased by members of each group), but found they all closely resembled figures for the national Consumer Price Index.[15]

This is not to say that the relative incomes of different occupational groups have not changed. Indeed, in a few instances changes have been quite large. For example, in the last decade the wages of machinists and other skilled workers have risen much faster than the rate of inflation, while wages of other groups, particularly university professors, have lagged considerably behind. Such changes primarily reflect the nature of the respective labor markets, the degree to which different occupations are unionized and bargain collectively, and other factors. They would occur regardless of whether the inflation rate were high, low, or zero. Nor does the evidence from these economic studies imply that inflation has not had a differential impact upon individuals *within* a given demographic or socioeconomic group: an individual who took out a 9% fixed rate mortgage on a house in California in 1975 would, *ceteris paribus*, be in substantially better financial shape than an equally wealthy individual who bought municipal bonds instead. When people are divided into the categories social scientists (and politicians) are used to thinking about, however, these effects tend to cancel out.[16]

In short, results of the present analysis are entirely consistent with the findings of previous research. Marked differences exist between personal difficulties resulting from inflation and those associated with unemployment. There are substantial objective economic costs associated with unemployment, but these costs are concentrated disproportionately among lower-income and occupational groups, and are thus largely confined to a small subset of the electorate. The immediate short-term costs of inflation, however, are not objective income and wealth effects, but the more intangible costs of operating in a more uncertain economic environment. And at least as it has played out in the United States during the past several years, the impact of inflation has been roughly the same across different age, income, and occupational groups.

The Effect of Personal Economic Problems upon Voting in Presidential and Congressional Elections

The whole point of developing the personal economic problem indicators was to enable us to conduct a more compelling test of the personal experiences version of the policy-oriented hypothesis. In the following analysis of voting in the 1972-76 presidential and congressional elections, then, the probit equation for each election will include dummy variables for each of the five categories of economic problems which were coded. A reference group was thus composed of respondents who failed to cite an economic problem or reported no problems at all. The hypothesis, of course, is that voters who believe inflation is their worst personal economic problem will give relatively greater support to the Republicans, while those who cite unemployment related problems will be more likely to vote Democratic. As in the previous voting analysis, the family finances "better" and "worse" terms were included in the equations in order to register incumbency-oriented voting. As before, the Panel Model, used in the 1974 and 1976 elections, specifies previous vote terms; Cross-sectional Model 1, used in the 1972 elections, specifies nominal party identification dummies. Also as before, positive signs are pro-Republican, negative signs are pro-Democratic. Results are presented in tables 5.3 and 5.4.

A comparison of the figures in tables 5.3 and 5.4 with those from the previous analysis (reported in tables 4.1 and 4.2) reveals some important similarities. Estimates for the family finances "better" and "worse" terms were virtually identical, thus registering considerable support for the incumbency-oriented hypothesis in both presidential elections and in the 1976 congressional election. Second, in all five elections estimates for the unemployment terms were pro-Democratic; although none were significant at the .05 level, three of them (both presidential elections and the 1976 congressional) achieve significance at $p < .10$. Furthermore, the

Table 5.3   The Effect of Personal Economic Problems upon Voting in Presidential Elections, 1972-1976

Variable	1972 [a]	1976
Constant	.53/(.17)**	-.26/(.13)*
Republican	.85/(.20)**	.79/(.13)**
Democrat	-.79/(.18)**	-.71/(.15)**
Family finances better	.03/(.12)	.13/(.10)
Family finances worse	-.33/(.13)**	-.19/(.12)*
Inflation	.29/(.16)*	.03/(.11)
Declining real income	-.08/(.23)	-.03/(.21)
Unemployment related	-.35/(.29)	-.37/(.25)
Taxes	.14/(.23)	-.04/(.23)
General econ. problems	.06/(.14)	-.04/(.12)
$\hat{R}^2$	.39	.32
n	760	923

a. See note 17. * $p < .05$ ** $p < .01$

estimates were generally a little larger (i.e., more Democratic) than were estimates for the respective head of household currently unemployed terms.

The verdict on the inflation side of the policy-oriented hypothesis, however, is rather mixed. Although the estimates were generally more positive and thus more pro-Republican than estimates for the unemployment terms, they were usually barely distinguishable from the catch-all reference groups. The real bright spot, of course, was the 1972 presidential election. Those individuals who felt their worst personal economic problem was inflation were much more likely to vote for Nixon than were other voters. An effect of size .29 would increase the probability of a voter voting Republican, *ceteris paribus*, from 50% to over 61%. This effect is even more impressive when the strong support Nixon received from the electorate as a whole is taken into account.

Table 5.4 The Effect of Personal Economic Problems upon Voting in Congressional Elections, 1972-1976

Variable	1972	1974	1976
Constant	.01/(.17)	-.50/(.14)*	-.45/(.12)**
Republican	.83/(.19)**	1.13/(.13)**	1.20/(.14)**
Democrat	-.98/(.19)**	-.56/(.13)**	-.24/(.12)*
Family finances better	.04/(.13)	.03/(.13)	.34/(.12)**
Family finances worse	-.04/(.15)	.17/(.12)	-.14/(.13)
Inflation	-.10/(.17)	-.06/(.12)	-.18/(.13)
Declining real income	-.20/(.30)	-.28/(.18)	-.07/(.23)
Unemployment related	-.59/(.42)	-.23/(.29)	-.38/(.30)
Taxes	-.41/(.24)	***	.22/(.25)
General econ. problems	.06/(.16)	-.10/(.14)	.05/(.15)
$\hat{R}^2$	.44	.37	.32
n	645	863	689

* $p < .05$ ** $p < .01$ *** Not included in equation because of very low n.

These findings suggest an important qualification to the hypothesis under consideration. Voters concerned about various personal economic problems may act upon them in a policy-oriented manner, but such voting may be for or against specific candidates, and not just parties in general. In 1972, apparently, voters who viewed inflation to be a serious personal problem did not hold this against Democratic congressional candidates but they were wary of McGovern. This differential pattern of support is reasonable. To many voters his $1,000-for-everybody "demogrant" proposal probably sounded like printing a large new batch of money, and Democratic congressional candidates were about as likely to endorse this scheme as they were to favor acid, amnesty, and abortion. To be sure, this interpretation is speculative and perhaps unnecessary. What may be going on is simply more of the same pattern uncovered earlier, i.e., that economic variables exert much stronger effects upon voters' decisions in presidential elections than in congressional elections. Still, it seems entirely plausible that policy-oriented voting might often be candidate specific, especially when presidential candidates espouse views more extreme than those of the mainstream of their party.[18]

Finally, the decision to distinguish between references to inflation per se and declining real income appears to have been prudent. Estimates of the latter variable's effect are all pro-Democratic in direction, and four of the five are more pro-Democratic in direction than the respective estimates for inflation. The gain was an exceedingly modest one, however, as differences between the two are usually tiny: averaging across all five presidential and congressional elections, the means of the estimates were -.004 for inflation and -.132 for declining real income.

For the remaining sets of problems there is little to be said. Estimates for the effect of taxes as a perceived personal problem are erratic in direction, while those for the "general economic problems" category do not reliably differ from zero.

To a large extent, then, these findings recapitulate those of the previous voting analysis. Although there was not much evidence of it in congressional elections, voters at the presidential level clearly responded in an incumbency-oriented fashion to perceived changes in their (family's) financial situation. Second, individuals who personally experience unemployment or difficulties associated with unemployment appeared to vote in a policy-oriented manner by giving somewhat more support to Democratic presidential and congressional candidates. The major new finding uncovered in this analysis was the pro-Republican, policy-oriented voting in the 1972 presidential contest which occurred in response to personal concern over inflation.

Potential Problems in Estimation

The logical next step in this analysis, of course, would be to attempt to account for the findings of the voting analysis, identifying those factors which either promote or impede the influence personally experienced economic problems exert upon voters' decisions. Before moving on to this task, though, it makes sense to consider some possible estimation problems which might have affected the results.

Probably the most chronic problem in multivariate analyses of voting behavior is simultaneity bias deriving from rationalization. If voters' evaluations of a candidate influence their reports of their views on some issue, for example, estimates of the influence of that issue on their voting decisions will obviously be susceptible to bias. Previous research and common sense identify a number of conditions under which the problem of rationalization is exacerbated. Clearly, such problems are greatest when respondents are asked to report their views on:

1. Issues which they either know or care little about.[19]

2. Issues on which candidates either avoid taking positions or make only deliberately vague and ambiguous pronouncements.[20]

3. Where they stand on an issue vis-à-vis major candidates or or parties.[21]

4. How well the president is handling a given problem, or how well different parties or candidates would handle a given problem.

The present analysis has obviously steered clear of these more obvious pitfalls. There are probably few things most individuals know or care much more about than recent trends in their own economic fortunes or the particular economic problems which affect them personally. According to Page's analysis, it is in the area of domestic economic policy that the stands of the Republican and Democratic parties most clearly and reliably differ.[22] Most importantly, none of the questions from which the indicators of personal economic experiences were derived made any mention of a party or candidate. Although rationalization cannot be ruled out completely, it was almost certainly minimized.[23]

This does not imply that voters' partisanship and their responses to the economic variables must be completely uncorrelated for the analysis to be valid. Problems would arise, though, if this correlation were very high, e.g., if those individuals personally troubled by unemployment were virtually all Democrats to begin with, or their inflation-sensitive counterparts were among the most stalwart of Republicans. If so, the effects of partisanship and personal economic problems would be difficult to disentangle, and effects due to the latter might be seriously underestimated.

This proved not to be the case. To be sure, respondents' personal economic problems and partisan predispositions were related. Table 5:5, which utilizes 1976 cross-sectional data, shows that respondents who named taxes their worst personal economic problem were a good deal more Republican than average. Those who cited unemployment, on the other hand, were substantially more Democratic, as were those who referred to a declining real income. The partisan makeup of the groups which cited either inflation or general economic problems, though, differed little from that of the total sample.[24] The most reliable effects upon voting, then, came from the most distinctly partisan category of voters, i.e., those who were personally troubled by unemployment, even though the probit equations had taken voters' basic party attachments into account. Furthermore, the only major effect of simply dropping the party identification and previous vote terms from the equations is to give a small boost to estimates of the unemployment term. This deletion also results in the signs of the taxes variable becoming more consistently pro-Republican in direction, but has virtually no effect on any of the other indicators of personal economic difficulties.

On the other hand, one might also suspect that the apparent impact of personally experienced unemployment upon voters' decisions is spurious. As pointed out earlier, blacks, young people, and workers in blue-collar occupations experience considerably higher than average rates of unemployment. These groups have also been major constituents of the Democratic party. Thus the unemployment measures may have isolated a group of voters of relatively low socioeconomic status who would have voted strongly Democratic had they been unemployed or not; as Schlozman and Verba put it, for these individuals bouts of unemployment

Table 5.5   The Relationship of Personal Economic
Problems to Partisanship, 1976 (*in percentages*)

Most important personal economic problems	Party identification		
	Democrats	Independents	Republicans
Inflation	50.6	14.0	35.4
Declining real income	59.3	8.8	31.9
Unemployment related	61.9	11.8	26.3
Taxes	45.5	11.6	42.9
General economic problems	52.9	14.8	32.3
Noneconomic problems	49.7	15.9	34.4
No problem mentioned	46.5	12.7	40.8
Total	50.9	14.0	35.1

simply add "injury to insult."[25] Instead of "overcontrolling" for differences in long-term party loyalties, the party identification and previous vote dummies may have failed to account fully for differences in social background. Effects actually due to these variables would thus be registered by the unemployment terms with which they were correlated.

The data suggest that this problem was present, but only to a small extent. As indicated earlier, all analyses using Cross-sectional Model 1 were repeated using Cross-sectional Model 2, which replaced the party identification dummies with a battery of social background variables. Among other things, this battery included the respondent's race, age, occupation, education, and family income. It should thus eliminate the potential sources of spurious effects in the unemployment term. Indeed, a comparison of Model 1 results (reported earlier) with those produced under Model 2 (reported in appendix 3) reveals that estimates of the head of household's unemployment terms were generally a little smaller with Model 2. These slight reductions are no great cause for alarm. Furthermore, the reverse pattern was obtained in the 1972 elections when the subjective unemployment problems measure was specified—probit estimates were larger under Model

2 than under Model 1. In short, the electoral effects attributed to personally experienced unemployment and unemployment-related difficulties, though often quite modest in magnitude, appear to be genuine.

Factors Mediating the Political Impact of Personal Economic Problems

The analyses in this and in the previous chapter both provided support for the hypothesis that voting in response to personally experienced unemployment is policy-oriented. What prevents these problems from taking on major electoral significance, of course, is that such problems appear to be salient to only small numbers of people. This is not to say that few people are affected by unemployment. In all three waves of the 1972-76 Panel Study over 20% of the respondents who were in the labor force reported being out of work at least once during the previous year (these figures are quite consistent with data from the Bureau of Labor Statistics).[26] But as the findings of the previous chapter indicated, the salience of unemployment's harmful economic consequences and its impact upon voting appear to fade quickly once a spell of joblessness ended. Responses to the family finances question given by individuals whose family head was currently working but had been out of work were virtually identical to responses given by people whose family head had never been unemployed in the previous year. Furthermore, the pro-Democratic impact of unemployment upon voters' decisions appeared to be generally much stronger in the currently unemployed category.

Some additional evidence on this matter is displayed in table 5.6, which shows the extent to which actual experiences with unemployment are reflected in self-reported economic problems. First of all, the figures in table 5.6 strongly corroborate the findings reported earlier, which indicated that the salience of unemployment declines rapidly once a spell of joblessness has ended. As the data here show, fewer than 10% of the respondents whose family head was currently employed but had been out of work referred to unemployment as their most serious personal economic problem. The apparently rapid discounting of past unemployment problems is, because of the large number of people

Table 5.6   References to Unemployment as a Personal Problem as a Function of Objective Unemployment Experiences, 1972-1976

Head of household's objective employment status	Percent naming unemployment their worst personal economic problem[b]		
	1972	*1974*	*1976*
Currently unemployed	36.4 (22)	42.9 (35)	27.3 (66)
Temporarily laid off[a]	11.1 (18)	13.1 (38)	4.8 (42)
Employed, but had been out of work in the previous year	9.1 (132)	9.3 (150)	5.8 (206)
Employed, never out of work in the previous year	1.9 (675)	2.1 (901)	3.2 (1079)

a. Beginning with the 1972 CPS Election Study, the format of the unemployment questions allowed respondents to report that they (or their family head) were either currently unemployed or temporarily laid off. Although this would be a useful distinction to make in the voting analyses, the smallness of the category sizes dictated that the "temporarily laid off" responses be subsumed under the "currently unemployed" category.

b. The numbers in parentheses are the *n*s upon which the percentages are based.

so affected, the most important factor limiting the electoral impact of personally experienced joblessness. In the 1976 cross-section, for example, only 4.8% of household heads in the labor force were reported to be currently unemployed, only 3.0% were reported to be temporarily laid off, but 14.8% were reported to be currently unemployed during the pervious year. Not surprisingly, those respondents whose head of household was currently out of work were by far the most likely to name unemployment their worst economic problem. Only a minority of these respondents cited it, however—the figures ranged from 43% in 1974 to 27% in 1976. Although around 60% of respondents in these surveys were also heads of households, the analysis shown in table 5.6 presumably excluded a large number of respondents for whom unemployment would not be a serious hardship, e.g., young people desiring only seasonal employment, members of families with other wage earners, students, or mothers looking for part-time work. Given that their family's chief breadwinner was currently out of work, the percentage of these respondents to whom unemployment was a salient, pressing problem seems surprisingly low.

Undoubtedly a major reason for this, as discussed earlier, is that a large share of the people who are out of work receive unemployment compensation and other benefits.[27] Many unions also provide supplemental benefits to unemployed members. And many erstwhile unemployed workers often augment their incomes by doing occasional odd jobs in return for cash or other goods and services.

Perhaps a more important reason for the frequent lack of salience of unemployment among individuals whose family head is currently out of work is that in many occupations periodic bouts of unemployment are expected, and seen as a natural part of the job. Similarly, a lack of job security is often counterbalanced by relatively high wage rates. Employment in the construction industry is a prime example—a construction worker is virtually certain to be laid off from time to time, but while working makes more money than he would at most other jobs requiring comparable levels of training and education. To the extent periodic unemployment is expected and can be prepared for, its salience as a personal problem would decline.

There is another way expectations might be important in lessening the sting of current unemployment. Not only would joblessness seem less serious if it were a "normal" occurrence—it would also be less traumatic for those who expect to be working again soon. As table 5.6 shows, respondents who reported that their head of household was temporarily laid off cited unemployment much less frequently than those who reported their status as unemployed. Presumably this is because the former group was much more likely than the latter to expect renewed employment in the near future. Another feature of the data in table 5.6 which jibes with this interpretation is the evidence indicating that the salience of unemployment is influenced by the general state of the economy. Respondents whose head of household was currently unemployed or temporarily laid off cited unemployment much more frequently in 1974 than in 1976. This seems understandable, given that the outlook for renewed employment was probably much brighter in 1976, a period of recovery, than in late 1974, when the economy was rapidly plunging into a recession.

In summary, the major reason why personally experienced unemployment has such a limited electoral impact is that the salience of such difficulties is confined to such a small subset of the electorate. For a number of reasons, less than half of those individuals whose family head was currently out of work reported unemployment to be a pressing personal problem. Even more importantly, the salience of past joblessness quickly recedes.

As with unemployment, only small numbers of respondents referred to taxes as their most serious economic problem. Concern over taxes also failed to exhibit a consistent influence upon voting decisions: with one exception, estimates for this term were scattered closely about zero, and it is hard to know what to make of the pro-Democratic direction of the significant 1972 congressional election estimate (if anything, policy-oriented voting in response to taxes would presumably run in a pro-Republican direction). Things may well have been different in 1978, if the highly publicized "tax revolt" was indicative of widespread discontent over personal tax burdens. Unfortunately, the 1978 CPS survey did not include the personal problems questions, so there is no way to tell one way or the other.

Plenty of people, however, fell into the remaining categories, reporting inflation, a declining real income, or general, miscellaneous economic problems to be personally troublesome. Yet none of these various other economic difficulties exerted a clear, consistent effect upon voting. To be sure, inflation-sensitive voters gave Nixon a considerable boost in 1972, but this was the only real bright spot. What explains this absence of effects?

According to the arguments of Kinder and Kiewiet and of Sniderman and Brody, which were discussed in an earlier chapter, whether or not personal problems become politically significant depends on how such problems are perceived.[28] People may see economic problems which are troubling them as general and widespread, as something they share with many other people throughout society. To the extent they believe that their fortunes depend on the nation's economy—upon which governmental policies presumably have some influence—they will see their problems as politically relevant, and believe that the government could and should take action to alleviate them.[29] On the other hand, they may believe that their fortunes depend largely upon wholly idiosyncratic factors, i.e., their own physical, mental, and financial endowments, what sorts of financial responsibilities they have, or the success of the firm with which they are employed, which are not directly affected by public policy. To the extent that people perceive their problems to be rooted in the particular circumstances of their own life, according to Sniderman and Brody, they will display a strong "ethic of self-reliance," and will see it to be their own responsibility to deal with their problems as best they can. When this is the case, personal problems, no matter how troublesome, are politically irrelevant.

As was also indicated earlier, the findings of Feldman's study are quite consistent with this argument. He found that when asked to relate the reasons why their family's financial situation had gotten better or worse over the past year, most respondents did not refer to national economic trends or to government policies. The small minority who did, however, exhibited a much higher level of incumbency-oriented voting in the 1972 presidential election than did voters who reported only personal, idiosyncratic factors.[30] Sniderman and Brody's analysis of data from the 1972 and 1974 waves of the CPS panel study produced very similar findings. These two surveys included a follow-up question to the personal problem battery which asked:

> Do you think this [the respondents' most important personal problem] is something you have to work out on your own, or is there someone who ought to be helping you with this? . . . Who is that?

Answers to this question distinguished respondents who felt their problems were something they themselves should take care of from those who felt government (either a particular agency or government in general) should be helping them. The degree of perceived governmental responsibility varied considerably from category to category. On the whole, however, the neoconservatives' fear that the "welfare surge" (produced by an increasingly paternalistic government) was undermining people's sense of personal responsibility was unfounded. To the contrary, most Americans believed that they ought to take care of their personal problems by themselves, thus strongly supporting Sniderman and Brody's claim that the ethic of self-reliance was alive and kicking.

The ethic of self-reliance, then, would obviously serve to limit the electoral impact of personal economic problems. If someone believes governmental assistance is either unnecessary or inappropriate in helping them handle their problems, it seems highly unlikely that such problems would have much influence upon their choice in an election.[31]

Sniderman and Brody's findings, however, suggest that perceptions of governmental responsibility may vary a great deal from one type of problem to another. It thus seemed prudent to repeat their analysis, but with the coding scheme developed for the present study. Results are reported in table 5.7. The figures reported are the percentage of respondents in each category who believe that the government should help them cope with their most important economic problem.

Table 5.7   Perceptions of Governmental Responsibility by Type of Economic Problem, 1972 and 1974

Most important personal problem[a]	Percentage of respondents who believe government should be helping them[b]	
	1972	*1974*
Inflation	71.0 (124)	66.7 (426)
Declining real income	54.2 (48)	61.2 (116)
Unemployment related	43.8 (32)	41.2 (51)
Taxes	62.7 (51)	—[c] —
General economic problems	20.0 (160)	33.6 (238)
Noneconomic problems	19.2 (463)	16.2 (525)

a. The questions which asked respondents to indicate who, if anyone, should be helping them with their problems were asked only in reference to their most important personal problem. Thus the analysis could not be performed upon their most important personal *economic* problem, which was used in the voting analysis, and *n*s of the economic problem categories are slightly reduced. The 1976 survey did not include these equations.

b. The numbers in parentheses below are the *n*s upon which the percentages are based.

c. Not reported because of low *n*.

The differences which appear in table 5.7 are striking. Most respondents who referred to inflation, taxes, or a declining real income believed government should be combating the problem that they found personally troublesome.[32] Those who named unemployment were somewhat less likely to feel such assistance was warranted.[33] The vast majority of respondents who cited general or miscellaneous economic problems, however (like those whose worst problems were noneconomic in nature), saw their problems as something they should take care of on their own.

For the most part these differences make sense in light of Sniderman and Brody's reasoning. Complaints about bills, lack of money, and other general economic problems are in most cases probably a product of experiences which seem peculiar to one's own circumstances, e.g., failing to get an expected raise or promotion, having a child who needs braces, or owning a car which is in the repair shop more often than not. After all, what can the government do about a car that won't start or crooked teeth. The opposite is true with inflation. When people see food, fuel, or housing prices going up they know that prices are rising not just for themselves, but for everybody. They can see that their own experiences with inflation are symptomatic of a problem affecting the entire economy, and that there is little they as individuals can do about it. Consequently, most people who felt their worst economic problem was inflation believed the government should be trying to curb it.

The ethic of self-reliance, then, is only a partial explanation for the generally weak influence personal economic problems have upon individuals' voting decisions. After all, for a personal economic problem to affect voting systematically does not require every voter who is concerned about it to see the need for remedial action on the part of the government. In the problem area in which personal difficulties affected voting most consistently, i.e., unemployment, perceptions of governmental responsibility were less widespread than in the inflation and taxes categories. Evidently the significant minority of unemployment-sensitive voters who did feel the government should be helping them were enough for the effects associated with this problem to show up in the voting analysis.

However, something more than the belief that public policies should be implemented to ameliorate personal difficulties with inflation, unemployment, or other economic problems is required for such problems to produce policy-oriented voting. It also requires, as was pointed out in the introductory chapter, that voters perceive differences between the parties and/or presidential candidates in the amount of effort and/or skill they would apply in combating these problems. If a voter believes both parties or candidates are equally (un)able to reduce inflation, for example, personal difficulties with inflation will not affect his choice between them.

Data from the 1972 CPS survey provide some evidence on this point. Respondents who stated that the government should help them with their worst personal problem were asked:

> Which political party do you think would be most likely to get the government [or government agency mentioned] to be helpful on this problem?

Besides naming either the Democrats or the Republicans, respondents could report that they saw no difference in the parties' ability or willingness to help them. In turn, these respondents could be distinguished from those who saw no need for the government to help them.

Table 5.8 reports the size of these various groups in each of the problem categories. The information it conveys goes a long way toward suggesting why the results of the voting analysis came out as they did. Although most respondents who had cited inflation believed the government should lend them a helping hand, about half of those who did also believed that neither party was more likely than the other "to get the government to be helpful" with their problem. Those who did see a difference between the parties gave a slight net advantage to the Democrats; given the small number of respondents involved, however, this narrow edge is of no real importance. Unfortunately, the CPS surveys did not ask respondents whether or not they would be more likely to receive assistance with their personal economic problems from a specific candidate. Such evidence would be very valuable in ascertaining whether the pro-Nixon effect associated with the inflation term in 1972 was genuine. Presumably a clear majority of voters in this category perceived a Nixon presidency as likely to be more helpful (or perhaps more accurately, a McGovern presidency to be more harmful) vis-à-vis inflation, even though they saw no differences here between the parties per se. Lacking evidence on this matter, however, there remains the nagging suspicion that what is actually responsible for this particular statistically signifi-cant effect is Type 1 error.[34]

Table 5.8   Perceptions of the Major Parties' Ability to Handle Economic Problems, 1972 (*in percentages*)[a]

Respondents' most important personal economic problems	No gov't action needed	No differ-ence between parties	Demo-crats better	Repub-licans better
Inflation	29.0	34.7	21.0	15.3
Declining real income	45.8	27.1	18.8	8.3
Unemployment related	56.2	15.6	25.1	3.1
Taxes	37.3	27.5	21.5	13.7
General economic problems	80.0	11.3	6.9	1.8
Noneconomic problems	80.8	11.9	4.3	3.0

a. Percentages are based upon the same *n*s as in table 5:7.

A similar pattern emerged for respondents who cited either taxes or a declining real income—those who perceived there to be a difference between the parties gave an edge to the Democrats, but only a small one. As was shown earlier, respondents who cited general or miscellaneous economic problems rarely believed that their difficulties warranted government action. The few that did gave no substantial support to either party—6.9% of the total felt they would be better served by the Democrats, while a trifling 1.8% believed the Republicans would be of more assistance.

The major exception to the main pattern of findings here concerned respondents in the unemployment category. Although the perceived degree of governmental responsibility was only moderate, the party differential was substantial. Fully one-quarter of the respondents who cited unemployment related problems felt they would fare better under the Democrats. Virtually none of them gave the edge to the Republicans. To be sure, because the personal problem questions were asked of only half the respondents in 1972, the resultant small size of the unemployment category ($n = 32$) raises some doubts about how robust this finding is. The figures here, however, are very close to those obtained by a question put to all respondents in the 1976 CPS survey which asked, "Which party would do a better job of dealing with unemployment?" About a third said the Democrats, while only 9% said the Republicans. Apparently, then, the reason why personally encountered unemployment has exerted a consistent influence over voters' choices in the elections since 1956 is due, to a large extent, to one simple fact—it is an area of policy in which they perceived a substantial difference in the competency and/or commitment of the two major parties.[35]

Summary

In order to allow a more refined test of the personal experiences version of the policy-oriented hypothesis, new measures of personally encountered difficulties with inflation, unemployment, and other economic problems were developed from responses to a set of open-ended questions included in the 1972 through 1976 CPS election studies. Analysis of these new measures produced findings which were quite consistent with those from a large number of previous studies. Above all, inflation and unemployment were found to differ greatly in the nature of the costs they entailed, and in the way in which their costs were distributed.

The voting analyses reported in this chapter did generate some support for this hypothesis. Those voters who cited unemployment as their most important personal economic problem appeared to give a modest but consistent boost to Democratic candidates. Voters who felt that inflation was the most serious economic problem they faced also provided Nixon with an impressive margin over McGovern in 1972. In the other four elections analyzed, inflation-sensitive voters voted Republican more often than voters in the unemployment category, but no more so than voters in the neutral, catch-all reference groups. The pattern of incumbency-oriented voting in response to ups and downs in family finances was virtually identical to what showed up in the previous analysis: there was evidence of it in presidential elections, but very little in congressional elections.

Finally, the data indicated that several factors serve to limit the electoral impact of personal economic problems. The importance of unemployment, of course, is limited by the small number of voters who are affected by it. The ethic of self-reliance deprived general economic problems of any punch. Most respondents who cited these problems believed they should take care of them on their own, and saw no need for the government to assist them. On the other hand, most people who felt plagued by either inflation or taxes did believe the government should be doing something about it. But they did not view either party as significantly more likely than the other to bring about policies which would remedy these problems. The political consequences of a declining real income were, to some extent, limited by all three factors.

It is time to shift attention to some new hypotheses. Perhaps it is appropriate, then, that the analysis undertaken in the next chapter will ask voters to shift their attention as well. For it is not their own financial conditions that will be investigated, or the major economic problems which they themselves face, but rather their assessments of the nation's economic health, and what they see to be the major problems facing the country as a whole.

6
National Economic Assessments

As is the case with personal economic experiences, most research to date on national economic assessments has centered on incumbency-oriented voting. In testing this hypothesis, previous studies have relied primarily upon responses to a question included in most CPS national election studies since 1962, which asks:

> Now turning to business conditions in the country as a whole . . . would you say that at the present time business conditions are better or worse than they were a year ago?

In general, the results of these analyses have afforded this hypothesis an impressive level of empirical support. Employing a fairly simple model, Kinder and Kiewiet found that voters who felt that national business conditions had worsened were consistently more likely to vote against congressional candidates of the president's party than voters who believed conditions had improved.[1] The evidence appears to be similarly supportive in senatorial races, as well as for presidential elections.[2]

Evidence bearing upon the national assessments version of the policy-oriented hypothesis, as was pointed out in chapter 2, comes from studies by Tufte and by Schlozman and Verba.[3] This hypothesis fared well in both studies: compared to other voters, those individuals who felt inflation was the more serious national economic problem cast a considerably higher percentage of ballots for the Republican candidate, while voters who believed the more important national economic problem was unemployment gave more support to the Democrat. Both studies, unfortunately, concerned only the 1976 presidential election, and so there is no way of knowing whether this same pattern appeared in other elections.

The purpose of this chapter is to conduct as systematic a test as possible of the national assessments version of both the incumbency-oriented and policy-oriented hypothesis. The other key concern of this analysis, of course, is to compare the empirical merits of these hypotheses with the personal experiences hypotheses. To assure that this comparison is a fair one, it is imperative to develop indicators of general assessments of the nation's economy and concern over specific national economic problems which are as similar to the personal economic experiences indicators as possible. As far as incumbency-oriented voting is concerned, the national business conditions item is a good counterpart to the family finances item—instead of asking about trends in the respondents' own economic conditions, it simply asks about the recent performance of the nation's economy. It also proved to be not exceedingly difficult to obtain suitable national-level counterparts to the personal economic problems measures used earlier. Except for the 1962 study, all CPS national election surveys administered from 1958 on contained questions which could be adopted for present purposes. Like the personal problems questions, these questions were both open-ended and nondirective. Respondents were simply asked to name the problems they believed were most serious—not for their own lives, in this case, but for the nation as a whole. Second, these questions did not refer to any parties, issues, or candidates. As before, rationalization cannot be ruled out completely, but this type of question should have kept it to a minimum.

The actual questions used were as follows:

What do you think are the most important problems facing this *country*? (1972, 1974, 1976, 1978)

What do you personally feel are the most important problems which the government in Washington should try to take care of? (1966, 1968, 1970)

What would you personally feel are the most important problems the government should try to take care of when the new president and Congress take office in January? (1960, 1964)

Now, how about problems here at home inside the United States in the past year or so . . . would you say that things in general have been going along better than they were a year ago, not as well as before, or have they stayed about the same? How is that? (1958)

As with their personal economic problems, indicators of respondents' perceptions of important national economic problems could be derived from their answers to these questions. This time it was unnecessary to recode the verbatim responses from the interview protocols: in every study the CPS national problem codes were sufficiently detailed and extensive to be used in creating the categories analyzed in the present study.

It was again possible to distinguish references to several other important economic problems in addition to unemployment and inflation. The resultant coding scheme and marginal frequencies for each year are presented in table 6.1. What are reported are the most important *economic* problems respondents cited; if a non-economic problem (e.g., crime) was deemed most important, but an economic problem was also mentioned, the economic problem was the one which was coded.[4]

Most of the categories require little explanation. The *inflation* category includes all those who named high or rising prices the most troublesome national economic problem. Occasionally they referred to particular goods or services, but most references concerned prices in general. Included under *unemployment* are the respondents who felt the government should create more jobs, provide job retraining, or grant aid to depressed areas; most, though, simply cited unemployment.

As the figures in table 6.1 clearly show, the number of respondents who named either of these two economic problems the most important closely tracked the actual inflation and unemployment rates in these years. The unemployment figures peaked in 1958 and 1976, as did the official rates of unemployment. Similarly, the percentage citing inflation as the most important national economic problem rose right along with prices during

Table 6.1   Most Important National Economic
Problems, 1958-1980, (*in percentages*)[a]

Problem reported	1958	1960	1964	1966	1968	1970
Inflation	6.4	3.7	1.2	15.9	2.6	14.2
Unemployment	33.9	11.6	6.9	2.6	2.3	7.9
Taxes	—	4.7	4.3	6.4	3.7	6.1
More govt. programs	—	20.3	27.3	19.8	16.1	26.1
Less govt. spending	—	3.5	3.6	7.2	2.5	1.9
General econ. problems	—	2.9	0.6	1.9	0.8	4.9
Noneconomic problems	18.2	42.1	37.9	38.5	69.4	34.6
No problem mentioned	41.5[b]	11.2	18.2	7.7	2.6	4.4
n	1514	1514	1571	1291	1557	1580

Problem reported	1972	1974	1976	1978	1980
Inflation	20.0	50.2	30.3	52.2	40.4
Unemployment	6.3	6.6	32.1	4.6	12.4
Taxes	5.5	0.3	1.6	2.5	2.1
More govt. programs	10.9	1.7	4.2	3.3	10.1
Less govt. spending	3.3	1.0	2.3	2.6	5.2
General econ. problems	8.0	26.5	14.1	6.3	11.8
Noneconomic problems	42.7	10.8	9.3	23.8	15.2
No problem mentioned	3.3	2.9	6.1	4.7	2.8
n	1109	1624	1217	2304	1391

a. Columns may not add exactly to 100% because of rounding error.   b. The "no problem mentioned" category in 1958 is not comparable to the same category in the other years. See note 4 for details.

the 1970s. There are not enough data here to bring any new evidence to bear upon the question of precisely how public opinion responds over time to movements in the inflation and unemployment rates. Even if there were it is unlikely that there would be anything much to add to the findings of Hibbs's study of this problem.[5] As indicated in chapter 2, other researchers who analyzed these measures also found that individuals' perceptions of important national problems clearly reflected events and conditions in the real world.[6] To be sure, the frequency with which inflation and unemployment was cited as a personal economic problem also moved up and down with the objective rates (see table 5.1). The point is, though, that perceptions of national problems are just as responsive to actual conditions as individuals' own personal experiences. Furthermore, in all three years in which comparisons are possible (1972, 1974, 1976), the number of respondents who cited inflation or unemployment at the national level was always much larger than the number who named either as their most serious personal problem. As shown in the previous chapter, the major factor limiting the electoral effects of personal unemployment difficulties was that these difficulties were salient to only a small number of voters. The potential effects of perceptions of unemployment as a national problem are thus much greater, especially in years like 1958 and 1976, when it was cited more frequently than any other problem.

Very few respondents, on the other hand, felt that *taxes* were the most important national economic problem. In 1972, 1974, and 1976, in fact, more respondents cited taxes at the personal level than at the national. Surprisingly, the percentage of respondents in the taxes category was smaller in 1978—a year which saw tax limitation referenda on the ballot in California, Michigan, and several other states—than in most years. And as was the case with the personal problems reports, it was not possible to ascertain which particular taxes respondents were referring to.

The next two categories each subsumed a wide range of responses. Under the heading of *need more government programs* were respondents who believed that the federal government should do more to alleviate social problems. Most of them advocated new or enlarged federal programs in particular areas: education, housing, transportation, health and medical care, urban renewal, poverty programs, aid to minorities, or social security.[7] The category also included those who felt that the government should increase its spending in order to stimulate the economy, and those who felt government should exert more control or regulatory power over private business. Regardless of the specific social ill respondents cited, then, what put them in this category was their belief that the role of the public sector should be expanded in order to remedy it.

Those individuals in the next category, however, believed that a large and growing public sector was precisely what was wrong with this country. A variety of responses fell under the rubric of *need less government spending*—the federal government's budget deficits, a lack of fiscal responsibility, waste and inefficiency in the bureaucracy, creeping socialism, the undermining of individual initiative by too many "giveaway" programs, or too much government interference in private enterprise. What respondents in this category shared, then, was the desire to see the government's power—especially its spending power—reduced.

As table 6.1 shows, this category was never a very large one, ranging from virtually zero in some years to a high of 7.2% in 1966. This came, incidentally, exactly two years after the percentage in "need more government programs" hit its peak. Evidently the 1964 mandate for a Great Society was not especially long-lived. Indeed, except for a resurgence in 1970, the size of the "need more government programs" category shrank steadily from that point on. Undoubtedly some of the decline is due to the change in question wording which occurred in 1972. Asking respondents to name the most important problems "the government in Washington should try to take care of" probably elicited more calls for new and larger federal programs than asking them to name the most important problems "facing this country." But the question wording change does not account for the drop which occurred after 1972. It seems likely that most people view inflation, unemployment, or the general state of the economy as prior concerns, which, as the economy stumbled through the seventies, took precedence over questions about the need for additional government programs.[8]

The central hypotheses to be tested in this chapter, of course, concern inflation and unemployment: voters who believe that the former is the most important national economic problem are predicted to give relatively greater support to Republican candidates; those concerned about the latter should tend to support the Democrats. Another traditional point of contention between parties of the Left and Right, however, concerns the proper size of the public sector: parties of the Left favor its expansion, parties of the Right oppose it.[9] Tufte presents evidence indicating that even the "ideologically bland" parties of the U.S. differ on this score.[10] The national economic problems data can be used to determine whether this difference is also present in the parties' electoral bases of support. The analysis to follow, then, will test a second set of policy-oriented hypotheses: voters who believe that more government programs are needed to remedy serious national problems should give relatively greater support to Democrats; Republican candidates, however, should garner relatively more support from voters who believe the opposite—that the nation's worst problem is too much government spending. Similarly, voters who wish to see the extractive power of government reduced, i.e., those who name taxes as the nation's worst economic problem, might be expected to vote Republican more often as well. Although "taxes" and "need less government spending" were distinct—the latter was composed mostly of references to waste, deficits, and opposition to welfare—to some extent they are two sides of the same coin.

Most respondents in the next category, *general or miscellaneous economic problems,* were subsumed under the "general" heading, referring simply to "the economy." The miscellany included those who cited interest rates, the balance of payments deficit, the need to return to the gold standard, or a bearish stock market. Only a handful of respondents mentioned these sorts of problems, however. The entire category, in fact, was quite small throughout the prosperous 1960s. The 1970s, though, were a different story: over a quarter of the respondents in the 1974 study were included in this category, as were over 10% in both 1976 and 1980. As was also the case at the personal level, no obvious policy-oriented hypotheses can be made about respondents who cited general or miscellaneous economic problems. They might be predicted to be more likely to vote against the incumbents, but at any rate this group is not central to the analysis.

Noneconomic problems, of course, include everything else: racial unrest, crime in the streets, the Vietnam War, foreign affairs, and a host of other things. Not surprisingly, this catch-all category was largest in the tumultuous, war-torn, but prosperous year of 1968, smallest in the peaceful but economically troubled period beginning in 1974. The last category, finally, is made up of respondents who did not mention any problems. This category was rarely a large one, and in the three years in which comparisons are possible (1972, 1974, and 1976) the percentage of people who failed to cite any national problems was considerably smaller than the percentage who failed to report any personal problems.

The Relationship between Personal Economic Experiences and National Economic Assessments

In testing the personal experiences and national assessments versions of the incumbency-oriented hypothesis, Kinder and Kiewiet reasoned that people's perceptions of the state of the national economy might be strongly colored by their own financial fortunes. Those who had been doing well recently would likely be bullish on the economy as a whole, while those who had been doing poorly would take a darker view of the economy's recent performance.[11]

The degree to which this proved not to be the case was striking. Kinder and Kiewiet found that individuals' perceptions of recent trends in national business conditions were only weakly correlated with their reports of how well they and their family had been doing lately (gammas clustered around the .2 level). Several analyses by Sears and his associates have also shown perceptions of national or social problems (or policy preferences) to be remarkably independent of direct, personal experiences with these problems in a number of different contexts, e.g., the Vietnam War, the 1974 oil embargo and resultant long lines at gas stations, and busing for the purpose of school desegregation.[12]

The results of a more extensive analysis of perceived trends in national business conditions are reported in table 6.2 (although these data are from 1980 only, results from other years were very similar). The numbers to the left in each entry are the probit estimates, those to the right the standard errors. The trichotomous business conditions measure was coded in such a way that positive signs indicate a greater probability of reporting that national business conditions had worsened in the past year.[13] The independent variables included the two directional party identification dummies, the family finances and head of household unemployment dummies which were used in previous analyses, two dummies derived from a question concerning the personal impact of

Table 6.2 Perceived Trends in National Business Conditions, 1980

Constant	.71/(.15)**
Democrat	-.07/(.09)
Republican	.25/(.10)**
Family finances better	.03/(.08)
Family finances worse	.22/(.08)**
Head unemployed currently	.19/(.16)
Head unemployed last year	-.04/(.11)
Inflation - no personal harm	-.30/(.08)**
Inflation - great personal harm	.08/(.08)
Professional-technical	-.14/(.12)
Managerial	.09/(.12)
Clerical-sales	-.11/(.10)
Skilled worker	-.07/(.12)
Unskilled worker	-.11/(.11)
Service	-.04/(.13)
Farmer	.47/(.33)
Black	.08/(.09)
Union	-.05/(.07)
Family income	.03/(.02)**
Education	.03/(.02)**
Pre-New Deal	.09/(.13)
New Deal	.08/(.09)
South	.21/(.07)**
Midwest	.36/(.09)**
Far West	.39/(.09)**
$\hat{R}^2$	.09
n	1614

** $p < .01$ * $p < .05$

inflation,[14] and dummies registering respondents' occupation, race, union membership, income, educational attainment, age cohort, and region of residence.

Consistent with Kinder and Kiewiet's findings, respondents who believed that their family finances had worsened were also somewhat more likely to feel that national business conditions had worsened; those who claimed not to have been personally harmed by inflation, on the other hand, were less likely to feel that the economy had worsened. Republicans also assessed business conditions more unfavorably, as did people with higher incomes, more education, and, apparently, farmers (the probit estimate for farmers was pretty large, but because there were so few farmers the standard error was large as well).

The regional effects present are a little surprising: compared to those in the reference group (an amalgam of people from the Northeast, Border States, and Rocky Mountain states), respondents from the South, Midwest, and Far West were more likely to perceive the economy to have declined over the previous year. It had seemed more likely beforehand that the regional dummies would register a "Sunbelt" effect, with people from the South and Far West (mainly Californians) having more favorable impressions of the course the economy had taken. But this was not the case.

The most impressive thing about table 6.2, however, is that the entire array of independent variables accounts for a meager .09 in $\hat{R}^2$. In data analysis a poor fit is usually bad news. Here it is not, however, for if a great deal of the cross-sectional variation in response to this question were due to personal, local, or subnational factors, the validity of this item as an indicator of general assessments of the *nation's* economy would certainly be called into question. A legitimate point, of course, is that if the national business conditions item is registering perceptions of the same object, i.e., the economy, why is there any cross-sectional variation at all? It would be quite unreasonable, though, to expect complete consensus. The performance of the economy, after all, is rarely unambiguously good or bad. Moreover, major indicators of economic health rarely move monotonically upward or downward over the course of an entire year, and so slight differences in retrospective time frames might easily lead to different assessments. In short, the general state of the economy is something about which reasonable people can and do, to some extent, disagree.

As the data in figure 6.1 illustrate, however, it is also true that massive swings in overall perceptions of the national economy occur in response to objective economic conditions. The points plotted are the means of responses to these survey questions, with "better" coded +1, "same" coded 0, and "worse" coded -1. The most favorable assessments, accordingly, occurred in 1964, while in the disastrous year of 1974 about 90% of the respondents felt that business conditions had gone downhill. Figure 6.1 also shows, as indicated earlier, that responses to the family finances item move up and down with the economy in general, but to a much more limited extent. This is exactly what should be expected, of course; many people do well financially even in bad years, while many others suffer financial reversals even in the best of years. The much greater interelection change in general assessments of the economy implies, of course, that the potential effects of these assessments upon election outcomes are much greater than effects associated with personal economic conditions.

Figure 6.1
Trends in Family Finances and National
Business Conditions, 1960-1980[a]

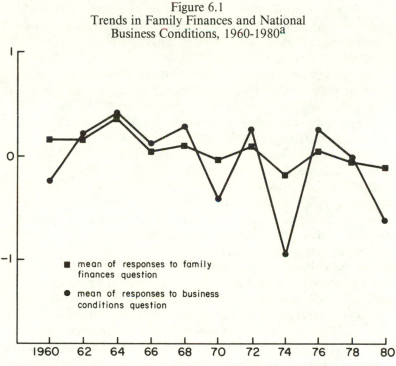

a. Data on perceptions of national business conditions are taken from the Minor Election Study in 1960, the first quarter 1965 Survey of Consumer Finances for 1964. and the first quarter 1975 Survey of Consumer Finances for 1974. All other data are taken from the CPS National Elections Studies.

What has not been examined yet is the extent to which the national economic problem perceptions are influenced, in the cross-section, by subnational factors. Thus the analysis performed upon the business conditions measure was repeated upon the dummy variables formed by the categories of respondents who named unemployment or inflation as the nation's most important economic problem. These variables take on the value of 1 if the respondent fell into the relevant category, 0 otherwise. Thus positive signs indicate a higher probability of citing the particular problem. The results are reported in table 6.3.

As these data show, there are a number of variables which tend to heighten or to dampen the salience of these two problems. Democrats, clerical and sales workers, blacks, and respondents who named unemployment their most serious personal economic problem were somewhat more likely than average to refer to unemployment, while older people, those with more education, Southerners, and farmers were somewhat less likely. Similarly, respondents who referred to inflation as a personal economic problem were also more likely to cite it at the national level, as were individuals in the "declining real income" category. There were also a few demographic variables which affected the propensity of individuals to refer to inflation.

In short, respondents who possessed certain socioeconomic or demographic characteristics, or who were personally troubled by inflation or unemployment, were more likely to believe these respective problems were nationally troublesome. The strength of these associations, though, should not be overstated. Cross-tabular analyses of these data showed that the vast majority of individuals who named inflation or unemployment as the nation's most serious economic problem in 1976 had not reported them to be personal problems. The $\hat{R}^2$s in table 6.3, moreover, are nearly as low as in table 6.2. The pattern of results here is thus quite similar to that which emerged from the analysis of the business conditions measures. There is some cross-sectional variation, but direct personal exposure to different economic problems and a rather standard array of background socioeconomic and demographic variables do not account for a large amount of it. In contrast, changes in objective national economic conditions provoke massive shifts in the distribution of responses to the national business conditions and most important national problems questions. This study can thus proceed with a great deal of confidence in the validity of the national assessments measures which have been developed.

Table 6.3   Perceptions of Unemployment and Inflation as
Important National Economic Problems, 1976

Variable	Unemployment	Inflation
Constant	-.31/(.15)**	-.01/(.18)
Democrat	.36/(.09)**	-.05/(.09)
Republican	.06/(.10)	.07/(.10)
Inflation	-.12/(.08)	.46/(.08)**
Declining real income	-.05/(.13)	.28/(.13)*
Unemployment	.39/(.16)**	-.27/(.19)
Taxes	-.09/(.16)	-.40/(.19)*
General econ. problems	-.12/(.08)	.11/(.09)
Professional-technical	-.00/(.12)	.05/(.12)
Managerial	-.16/(.12)	-.18/(.12)
Clerical-sales	.15/(.09)*	-.13/(.10)
Skilled worker	.03/(.11)	-.11/(.12)
Unskilled worker	.16/(.11)	-.13/(.12)
Service	-.01/(.11)	.10/(.11)
Farmer	-.38/(.20)*	-.05/(.19)
Black	.24/(.10)**	-.35/(.12)**
Family income	-.01/(.01)	.02/(.01)
Education	-.03/(.02)*	.02.(.02)
Pre-New Deal	-.17/(.11)*	-.01/(.11)
New Deal	-.20/(.08)**	.12/(.08)
South	-.26/(.09)**	.14/(.09)
Midwest	-.11/(.08)	.16/(.08)*
Far West	-.07/(.09)	-.07/(.10)
$\hat{R}^2$	.11	.09
n	1921	1921

* $p < .05$ ** $p < .01$

One final matter must be addressed before we move on to the
voting analysis, and that is the relationship between general
assessments of the nation's economy and perceptions of specific
national economic problems. In most election years the strength
of the correlation between them is not of major concern, in that
both sets of measures are available and can be specified in the

same probit equation. Unfortunately, five of the twelve CPS election studies between 1958 and 1980 (1958, 1960, 1964, 1970, and 1974) failed to include the national business conditions question. And although the 1972 election study included both questions, it too is problematic. Because of a number of constraints, the survey undertaken that year was divided into two parts (Form I and Form II), and each part was administered to half the respondents. Many questions appeared on both forms, but many did not. In particular, the national business conditions question appeared on Form I only, while the most important national problems question was present only on Form II. It is thus impossible to specify both sets of variables in the same probit equation.

The potential problem, of course, is that if there is a strong relationship between general assessments of the nation's economy (which are hypothesized to result in incumbency-oriented voting) and perceptions of specific national economic problems (which are hypothesized to provoke policy-oriented voting), failing to specify measures of the former could result in measures of the latter picking up effects which are actually due to incumbency-oriented voting. The danger of this sort of bias would probably be highest when either unemployment or inflation was the dominant economic problem.[15]

Fortunately, the cross-tabulation displayed in table 6.4 strongly suggests that this problem is not a serious one. Although 12% of the respondents in 1980 did name unemployment to be the most important national economic problem, inflation, referred to by 40% of the respondents, was clearly uppermost in the public's mind. But as the data in table 6.4 indicate, respondents citing inflation reported general assessments of the nation's economy which were virtually identical to those reported by respondents in the unemployment category. To be sure, respondents in both categories gave slightly more unfavorable ratings of the economy than average. The important thing, though, is that people who referred to inflation instead of unemployment did not systematically take a gloomier view of the economy. Failing to specify the national business conditions measures in certain election equations, then, should not bias estimates of policy-oriented voting associated with the indicators of perceived national economic problems.

Table 6.4   The Relationship between General Assessments of
National Business Conditions and Perceptions of
Specific National Economic Problems, 1980

Most important national economic problem	National business conditions compared to a year ago			
	Better	Same	Worse	*n*
Unemployment	14.5	9.2	76.3	173
Inflation	11.9	13.0	75.1	562
Taxes	10.3	20.7	69.0	29
More govt. programs	13.6	22.9	63.6	140
Less govt. spending	16.7	20.8	62.5	72
General econ. problems	14.6	16.5	68.9	164
Noneconomic problems	9.0	25.0	66.0	212
No problem mentioned	15.4	30.8	53.8	39
Total	12.6	16.8	70.6	1391

National Assessments and Voting: Presidential Elections

The following analysis will proceed in much the same fashion as the previous ones. The Panel Model, used in the 1958, 1960, 1974, and 1976 studies, specifies previous vote terms. Cross-sectional Models 1 and 2, used for all other elections, specify nominal party identification dummies and a battery of socioeconomic and demographic variables, respectively. As before, results reported in the text are from Cross-sectional Model 1, while estimates derived from Model 2 are reported in appendix 3. Each equation also includes the personal economic experiences indicators which were used in the previous analyses, i.e., the family finances "better" and "worse" dummies, the most important personal economic problem dummies in 1972, 1974, and 1976, and the head of household's unemployment terms in all other years.

For the years in which the national business conditions question was included on the CPS survey, dummy variables analogous to the family finances terms were constructed. One was formed by the group of voters who felt conditions were better than they were a year ago, the other by those who thought things were worse, with those who felt conditions were about the same as a year ago forming the reference group. The hypothesis, of course, is that voters who believed national business conditions had improved would tend to give greater support to the incumbent presidential candidate, but those who believed they had worsened would tend to oppose him.

Similarly, dummy variables were created for each of the six types of perceived national economic problems which were coded. A reference group was thus formed by those who failed to cite an economic problem or who reported no problems at all. The policy-oriented hypotheses, again, were that individuals who named unemployment the most important national economic problem, or who believed that new or larger government programs were needed to address other national problems should vote more Democratic; voters who believed that the nation's most important problem was either inflation, taxes, or too much government spending should give relatively greater support to Republicans.

The results of this analysis are presented in table 6.5. As before, the left numbers in each entry are probit estimates and the number in parentheses to the right are standard errors. Democratic votes were coded 0 and Republican votes 1, so negative signs are pro-Democratic and positive signs pro-Republican.

Probably the first thing which should be said about table 6.5 is that almost all personal economic experience terms were little affected by the inclusion of the national economic assessments measures. The 1976 personal unemployment measure slipped slightly, but all other estimates were virtually identical to what they had been in the previous analyses. This provides considerable assurance as to the stability of the estimates for these terms. More importantly, it attests to the fact that the distinction between personal economic experiences and national economic assessments is not just a scholarly nicety, but a distinction which also exists in the minds of the voters. The findings of the previous voting analyses thus remain intact: the family finances measures register modest incumbency-oriented effects; personal exposure to unemployment exerts a consistently pro-Democratic influence,

Table 6.5 National Economic Assessments and Voting:
Presidential Elections, 1958-1980

Variable	*1960*	*1964*	*1968* [a]
Constant	-.04/(.09)	-.57/(.18)**	.52/(.18)**
Republican	.59/(.09)**	1.29/(.19)**	1.02/(.19)**
Democrat	-1.07/(.11)**	-.53/(.18)**	-1.26/(.17)**
Personal economic experiences			
Family finances better	.14/(.09)	-.03/(.10)	-.33/(.12)**
Family finances worse	-.05/(.12)	.18/(.15)	.14/(.15)
Head unemployed currently	-.6l/(.31)*	-.83/(.70)	.05/(.47)
Head unemployed last year	-.24/(.19)	-.56/(.34)*	.02/(.37)
Inflation	—	—	—
Declining real income	—	—	—
Unemployment	—	—	—
Taxes	—	—	—
General economic problems	—	—	—
National economic assessments			
Business conditions better	—	—	.10/(.12)
Business conditions worse	—	—	.30/(.19)
Unemployment	-.24/(.14)*	-.22/(.19)	.28/(.29)
Inflation	.38/(.23)*	.51/(.49)	-.03/(.24)
Taxes	.07/(.20)	.2l/(.20)	.43/(.22)*
More government programs	-.06/(.10)	-.52/(.11)**	-.20/(.12)*
Less government spending	-.17/(.21)	.36/(.22)*	.73/(.32)*
General economic problems	.09/(.22)	***	***
$\hat{R}^2$	.34	.48	.58
n	1149	1111	911

$* p < .05$ $** p < .01$ $***$ Not included in the equation because of low *n*.

Table 6.5   National Economic Assessments and Voting:
Presidential Elections, 1958-1980 (*continued*)

Variable	1972 [b]	1976	1980 [c]
Constant	.69/(.17)**	-.25/(.19)	.57/(.22)
Republican	.72/(.19)**	.67/(.13)**	.80/(.19)**
Democrat	-.82/(.17)**	-.73/(.15)**	-1.26/(.17)**
Personal economic experiences			
Family finances better	.05/(.12)	-.02/(.11)	-.15/(.14)
Family finances worse	-.30/(.14)*	-.19/(.12)	.13/(.14)
Head unemployed currently	—	—	-.85/(.32)**
Head unemployed last year	—	—	-.04/(.18)
Inflation	.27/(.16)*	-.01/(.12)	—
Declining real income	-.09/(.23)	-.01/(.21)	—
Unemployment	-.35/(.30)	-.24/(.27)	—
Taxes	.07/(.23)	.02/(.23)	—
General economic problems	.07/(.14)	-.08/(.13)	—
National economic assessments			
Business conditions better	.25/(.12)*	.53/(.11)**	-.14/(.19)
Business conditions worse	-.26/(.17)	-.15/(.13)	.33/(.14)**
Unemployment	.02/(.22)	-.40/(.15)**	-.50/(.20)**
Inflation	.04/(.14)	.08/(.15)	-.05/(.15)
Taxes	.36/(.26)	-.04/(.41)	.50/(.44)
More government programs	-.07/(.18)	.15/(.27)	-.34/(.21)*
Less government spending	.20/(.31)	.22/(.34)	-.07/(.25)
General economic problems	-.42/(.20)*	-.03/(.17)	-.16/(.19)
$\hat{R}^2$	.40	.40	.54
n	827	923	877

a. Wallace voters were excluded from the analysis in 1968. b. See note 16.
c. Anderson voters excluded from the analysis in 1980.
* $p < .05$ ** $p < .01$ *** Not included in the equation because of very low *n*.

but only upon the decisions of a small number of voters; and the evidence of policy-oriented, pro-Republican voting in response to the problem of inflation in the 1972 presidential election also persisted. The personal experiences version of both the incumbency-oriented and policy-oriented hypotheses, then, continues to receive some empirical backing.

Inspection of table 6.5 also shows that the data provide strong support for the national assessments version of both hypotheses. Signs of all but one of the estimates of the national business conditions terms were all consistent with the hypothesis that the more favorably individuals rated the recent course of the economy, the more likely they were to vote for the incumbent presidential candidates (and although the estimate of the aberrant 1968 "better" term was more anti-incumbent than the reference group, it was still more pro-incumbent than the estimate for the "worse" term). Moreover, in three of the four elections in which the measures were available the estimate of one of the pair was significantly different from the reference group. Statistical significance, of course, is not necessarily substantively important, but in this case the effect upon voting decisions registered by these measures was impressive in magnitude. The average of the distance between estimates of the business conditions "better" and "worse" terms was .47. An effect of this size would increase the probability that an individual would vote for (or against) the incumbent from 50% up to 68%. As was the case at the personal level, there did not appear to be any evidence here to support the asymmetric version of the incumbency-oriented hypothesis. Sometimes the "better" term was larger, sometimes the "worse" term was, but incumbent candidates did not seem to be punished any more than they were rewarded.

The .47 average difference between the pairs of business conditions terms is somewhat larger than the average .28 difference between the "better" and "worse" family finances terms. General assessments of the national economy thus appear to exert a stronger incumbency-oriented influence upon individual voters' decisions than do perceived trends in their own economic conditions. This pattern of evidence is quite in keeping with the findings of previous analyses which compared these two alternatives.[17]

The national assessments version of the policy-oriented hypothesis also fared well in this analysis. In 1960, 1976, and 1980, those who believed that the nation's most important economic problem was unemployment voted significantly more Democratic than did those who believed it was inflation. All three of these elections, of course, occurred in years in which unemployment and/or inflation was serious enough to be cited as a national problem by a large segment of the voting public. Conversely, in the prosperous year of 1968, when fewer than 3% of the voters referred to each of these problems, the hypothesis fared quite poorly. To be sure, there was no real difference between estimates of the national level inflation and unemployment terms in 1972, even though these problems were cited by a large percentage of the voters. This is particularly embarassing for the national assessments version, given that in this election personally encountered difficulties stemming from inflation and unemployment did appear to provoke policy-oriented voting. In general, though, in the years in which unemployment and/or inflation were high on the national agenda, these issues influenced voters' choices for president in the manner predicted by the poliy-oriented hypothesis.

The results reported in table 6.5 also gave substantial empirical backing to the auxiliary hypothesis concerning the proper size and scope of the public sector. With a couple of exceptions (the 1960 "less government spending" term and the 1968 "taxes" term), those who believed new or expanded government programs were needed to attack serious national problems voted Democratic more often than did individuals who believed instead that too *much* government spending or taxation was the most important problem facing the nation. As was the case with the unemployment-inflation hypothesis, the public sector hypothesis made its strongest showing in the election years in which a large segment of the electorate fell into the relevant categories. Here, though, they were the relatively prosperous years of 1964 and 1968. Estimates for most of the public sector terms in these years were significantly different from the reference group, and are indicative of large effects upon individuals' voting decisions. In 1964, for instance, the -.52 probit estimate associated with the "more government programs" term means that falling into this category would, *ceteris paribus*, increase the probability of an individual voting for Johnson from 50% to 70%. Holding the opposite opinion, that the nation's worst economic problem was too *much* government spending, would likewise lower the probability of an individual voting for Johnson, everything else being equal, from 50% to 36%.

But Goldwater's call for a major reduction in the role of the federal government in the American economy came at a strikingly unpropitious time. According to the evidence presented back in table 6.1, in 1964 the desire to combat poverty, racial inequality, and other social problems, the perceived efficacy of government programs to do so, and the belief that a strong economy could pay for these programs were at a very high level. The number of voters who believed serious national problems necessitated an expansion of the public sector was nearly eight times greater than the number who believed it was crucial to reduce government spending. It is easy to see, then, that on this issue Goldwater got the short end of the stick.[18]

The issue of whether the nation would be better served by a larger or smaller public sector also exerted a strong influence upon voters' choices in the 1968 presidential election. The evidence here is entirely consistent with previous analyses of that election. Although the Vietnam War was far and away the greatest source of popular concern, voters' policy preferences concerning future conduct of the war had little to do with their choice between Nixon and Humphrey. As Page and Brody demonstrated, the reason for this was simple: with few exceptions, the statements of both candidates on the war were mainly vague and ambiguous generalities, making it virtually impossible for voters even to determine what their positions were, let alone to distinguish between them.[19] On the question of the proper size and scope of the public sector, however, the story was quite different. Here the electorate was offered choices, not echoes. Consequently, the survey responses which were most strongly related to support for Humphrey or Nixon were to questions concerning whether or not the federal government should guarantee every American a job and good standard of living, whether or not it should increase funding of educational programs, whether or not it should expand its role in providing health care, and, above all, to a question asking whether or not "the government in Washington is getting too strong for the good of the country."[20]

The final category in table 6.5 to be considered was composed of voters who cited either the economy in general or a miscellany of other specific economic problems. For the most part the behavior of these voters did not differ from that of the reference group. Furthermore, in 1964 and 1968 this category was too small to be even specified in the probit equation. In 1972, though, voters in this category gave significantly more support than did those in the reference group to the Democratic challenger McGovern. Given the vague, general nature of the perceptions which fell into this category, it probably makes sense to view this one isolated effect as augmenting the incumbency-oriented voting registered by the national business conditions terms.

Congressional Elections

The results obtained from running this set of probit equations upon voting in congressional elections are reported in table 6.6. As before, the numbers on the left are the probit estimates, the numbers on the right the standard errors. Positive signs indicate a pro-Republican effect, negative signs a pro-Democratic effect.

As in the analysis of presidential elections, estimates of the personal economic experiences terms were generally not greatly perturbed by inclusion of the national assessments measures. As before, few estimates of the unemployment terms attained conventional levels of statistical significance (which is not surprising, given the frequently small n in these categories) but an overwhelming proportion of them (seventeen of twenty) were pro-Democratic in direction. Estimates of the family finances terms, on the other hand, were a good deal smaller on average and were more frequently in the wrong direction. The verdict at this level thus remains the same: personally experienced unemployment appears to exert a very modest but consistent pro-Democratic influence; the incumbency-oriented voting in congressional elections provoked by recent trends in family finances, however, is quite unimpressive in both magnitude and consistency.

There is, though, considerable support for the national assessments version of the incumbency-oriented hypothesis. In all seven years in which the data were available, estimates of the business conditions "better" terms were more pro-incumbent than estimates of the "worse" terms. In four of the seven cases the estimate of one of the pair of terms was significantly different from the reference group (composed of voters who felt national business conditions were about the same as a year ago), and in another election (1962) the "better" and "worse" terms were significantly

Table 6.6   National Economic Assessments and Voting:
Congressional Elections, 1958-1980

Variable	1958	1960	1962
Constant	-.26/(.12)*	-.21/(.09)*	-.30/(.21)
Republican	1.00/(.12)**	1.28/(.12)**	1.40/(.22)**
Democrat	-.96/(.13)**	-.76/(.10)**	-.94/(.21)**
Personal economic experiences			
Family finances better	.22/(.11)*	.03/(.10)	-.03/(.14)
Family finances worse	-.18/(.15)	-.07/(.13)	.07/(.17)
Head unemployed currently	-.45/(.40)	-.60/(.37)*	-.25/(.49)
Head unemployed last year	-.43/(.25)*	.03/(.23)	-.21/(.26)
Inflation	—	—	—
Declining real income	—	—	—
Unemployment	—	—	—
Taxes	—	—	—
General economic problems	—	—	—
National economic assessments			
Business conditions better	—	—	-.13/(.14)
Business conditions worse	—	—	.23/(.17)
Unemployment	-.30/(.11)**	.02/(.15)	—
Inflation	.01/(.21)	.17/(.27)	—
Taxes	—	.08/(.24)	—
More government programs	—	.20/(.12)*	—
Less government spending	—	-.05/(.23)	—
General economic problems	—	.18/(.24)	—
$\hat{R}^2$	.45	.42	.56
n	825	987	697

* $p < .05$ ** $p < .01$

Table 6.6 National Economic Assessments and Voting:
Congressional Elections, 1958-1980 *(continued)*

Variable	1964	1966	1968
Constant	-.68/(.21)**	.06/(.19)	-.19/(.17)
Republican	1.31/(.21)**	·.99/(.19)**	.99/(.18)**
Democrat	-.56/(.20)**	-.91/(.18)**	-.73/(.17)**
Personal economic experiences			
Family finances better	.08/(.11)	-.10/(.13)	.10/(.11)
Family finances worse	.07/(.16)	-.50/(.14)**	.27/(.14)*
Head unemployed currently	-.32/(.56)	-.74/(.57)	-.61/(.52)
Head unemployed last year	.20/(.27)	—	-.24/(.37)
Inflation	—	—	—
Declining real income	—	—	—
Unemployment	—	—	—
Taxes	—	—	—
General economic problems	—	—	—
National economic assessments			
Business conditions better	—	-.26/(.13)*	-.01/(.11)
Business conditions worse	—	.08/(.15)	.09/(.18)
Unemployment	-.02/(.19)	.76/(.32)	.54/(.28)*
Inflation	1.02/(.55)*	.34/(.17)*	.35/(.24)
Taxes	.32/(.22)	.17/(.25)	.37/(.20)*
More government programs	-.08/(.12)	-.03/(.15)	.09/(.11)
Less government spending	.55/(.23)**	-.09/(.20)	.54/(.24)*
General economic problems	***	.04/(.37)	***
$\hat{R}^2$	.46	.46	.43
n	957	677	871

* $p < .05$ ** $p < .01$ ***Not included in equation because of very low n.

Table 6.6   National Economic Assessments and Voting:
Congressional Elections, 1958-1980 *(continued)*

Variable	1970	1972	1974
Constant	-.07/(.18)	-.26/(.18)	-.53/(.19)**
Republican	1.09/(.19)**	1.04/(.19)**	1.13/(.13)**
Democrat	-.83/(.18)**	-.68/(.19)**	-.57/(.13)**
Personal economic experiences			
Family finances better	.04/(.20)	.02/(.13)	.03/(.13)
Family finances worse	-.01/(.19)	.08/(.16)**	.17/(.12)
Head unemployed currently	-.50/(.49)	—	—
Head unemployed last year	-.30/(.37)	—	—
Inflation	—	-.02/(.18)	-.06/(.12)
Declining real income	—	-.19/(.30)	-.28/(.18)
Unemployment	—	-.54/(.41)	-.26/(.29)
Taxes	—	-.39/(.25)	***
General economic problems	—	.09/(.16)	.07/(.14)
National economic assessments			
Business conditions better	—	.06/(.12)	—
Business conditions worse	—	-.32/(.19)*	—
Unemployment	.18/(.22)	.07/(.25)	.00/(.23)
Inflation	-.21/(.17)	-.28/(.16)	.00/(.15)
Taxes	-.08/(.27)	-.12/(.26)	***
More government programs	.03/(.14)	-.14/(.18)	***
Less government spending	.42/(.38)	-.14/(.32)	***
General economic problems	-.05/(.23)	-.22/(.21)	.13/(.16)
$\hat{R}^2$	.45	.44	.37
n	683	692	883

* $p < .05$ ** $p < .01$ ***Not included in equation because of very low n.

Table 6.6   National Economic Assessments and Voting:
Congressional Elections, 1958-1980 *(continued)*

Variable	*1976*	*1978*	*1980*
Constant	-.48/(.19)**	-.10/(.19)	-.09/(.20)
Republican	1.15/(.14)**	.67/(.15)**	.81/(.17)**
Democrat	-.27/(.13)*	-.60/(.14)**	-.51/(.16)**
Personal economic experiences			
Family finances better	.23/(.13)*	-.13/(.11)	-.05/(.12)
Family finances worse	-.19/(.14)	-.19/(.10)	.07/(.12)
Head unemployed currently	—	-.25/(.32)	-.01/(.30)
Head unemployed last year	—	-.05/(.14)	.24/(.17)
Inflation	.21/(.14)	—	—
Declining real income	-.10/(.23)	—	—
Unemployment	-.21/(.32)	—	—
Taxes	.24/(.25)	—	—
General economic problems	.01/(.15)	—	—
National economic assessments			
Business conditions better	.27/(.13)*	-.08/(.11)	-.35/(.18)*
Business conditions worse	-.09/(.15)	.11/(.11)	-.01/(.13)
Unemployment	-.22/(.17)	-.31/(.26)	-.54/(.19)**
Inflation	.10/(.17)	.01/(.14)	-.29/(.14)*
Taxes	-.74/(.51)	.20/(.24)	.36/(.39)
More government programs	-.97/(.31)**	.49/(.25)*	-.41/(.20)*
Less government spending	-.14/(.36)	.20/(.23)	.06/(.23)
General economic problems	.15/(.20)	.14/(.18)	-.28/(.18)
$\hat{R}^2$	.37	.29	.32
n	689	1009	859

* $p < .05$ ** $p < .01$

different from each other. The average of the differences between estimates of the "better" and "worse" terms, furthermore, was a sizeable .30. In short, the findings here strongly corroborate those of previous studies by Kinder and Kiewiet, Ben-Gera Logan, and others. Voters who believe that conditions in the nation's economy have improved over the previous year are much more likely to cast their ballots for congressional candidates of the incumbent president's party than are voters who believe that national economic conditions have deteriorated.

The policy-oriented hypotheses, in contrast, did not fare nearly as well as they did in the presidential election analysis. To be sure, there are some bright spots. Estimates for the public sector terms generated by the 1964, 1968, and 1980 congressional election equations bear a rough but unmistakable resemblance to those of the respective presidential elections. In these years voters who believed that the nation was being jeopardized by a government which spent too much or taxed too much were much more supportive of the Republican presidential nominee than voters who felt that a variety of national problems warranted new or expanded federal programs to deal with them. As table 6.6 indicates, they were more likely to vote for Republican congressional candidates as well. Differences between estimates of the various terms are all pretty large in these years, with those of the "less government spending" terms in 1964 and 1968, the "taxes" term in 1968, and the "more government programs" term in 1980 significantly different from the reference group at the .05 level or better.

Similarly, there are some years when the inflation-unemployment policy-oriented hypothesis fares pretty well. The Republicans paid dearly for the 1958 recession: over a third of the voters in that year believed unemployment was the most important national economic problem, and they were significantly more likely to cast their ballots for Democratic congressional candidates. And in 1966 the large number of voters (16% of the sample) who cited inflation as the nation's worst economic problem were a good deal more likely than average to vote Republican. At the present juncture it seems hard to believe that the 2.8% rise in consumer prices that year triggered such a reaction, but this was a major spurt compared to the average 1.3% of the previous five years. And as Safire points out, the Republicans ran hard on the issue in 1966: one of their pieces of campaign literature was "a long paper in the shape of a supermarket cashier's tape with comparative food prices on it and a denuniciation of Johnson inflation."[21]

On the other hand, individuals who believed that inflation was the most serious national economic problem in 1966 did not vote as strongly Republican as the people who named unemployment. Given that the latter group was very small, this would not be especially troubling if it were not for the fact that estimates of the unemployment terms were also more pro-Republican than those of the inflation terms in 1964, 1968, 1970, and 1972. Similarly, there are a number of occasions (1960, 1976, and 1978) when estimates of the "more government programs" terms were not only more pro-Republican than those of the "less government spending" terms, but were also significantly more pro-Republican than the respective reference groups in these years.

There is some consolation in that there is a tendency here, similar to that in presidential elections, for the policy-oriented hypotheses to fare better in the election years in which the relevant problems were salient to large portions of the electorate. But enough estimates ran contrary to the hypotheses' predictions even then to permit a very favorable verdict. Although this analysis generated relatively strong support for the national assessments version of the incumbency-oriented hypothesis, voters' choices between congressional candidates of the two major parties do not appear to have been consistently influenced by what they perceived to be the nation's most important economic problems.

Perceptions of Governmental Responsibility for National Economic Problems

One of the factors identified in the previous chapter as dampening the influence of personal economic problems upon voting decisions is what Sniderman and Brody describe as the "ethic of self-reliance."[22] Table 5.7 demonstrated, however, that the degree to which people believed that the government should (or should not) help them deal with their most pressing problem depended heavily upon the type of problem they mentioned.

Most respondents who referred to vague, general economic problems felt that they themselves were primarily responsible for dealing with these problems as best they could. The vast majority of those who named inflation (or taxes), on the other hand, believed that the government should help them cope with their problems. Those who cited unemployment and related difficulties split about evenly between these alternatives.

According to Brody and Sniderman, these findings can be accounted for by differences in the perceived universality of these problems. By their line of reasoning, most ordinary economic problems—e.g., unexpected bills, a chronic lack of money, or being heavily in debt—are usually seen as rooted in one's peculiar circumstances, and of little relevance to anyone else. This is also apparently true, but to a lesser extent, of personal experiences with unemployment. The ethic of self-reliance does not stand up nearly so well in the face of inflation, however. When people see prices going up they know that prices are rising for everybody, not just for themselves, and that there is little that they, as individuals, can do about it. Most people, in short, appear to view their own difficulties with inflation as one particular instance of a problem which affects the American public in general.

When it comes to perceptions of national problems, though, such considerations should not be apropos. They are by definition problems which people see to be quite general and widespread. If Sniderman and Brody's reasoning is correct, people should assign to government a high degree of responsibility for ameliorating whatever national problem they hold to be most important.

Data from the 1976 CPS survey strongly support this conjecture. After respondents had indicated what they believed to be the most important problem facing the country, they were asked:

> How much responsibility should the government in general have in solving this problem—a great deal, some, or none at all?

Table 6.7 illustrates how responses to this question broke down according to the particular problem mentioned. As predicted, the degree of responsibility respondents assigned the government was very high, and differences between the various problem categories were not very large. Hardly any respondents believed the government had no role at all to play in solving the problem they cited, so the small differences present were between the size of the proportions who believed government had "some" responsibility versus "a great deal." Interestingly, percentages in the "great deal" column were somewhat higher when the perceived problem was the government doing too much—either too much spending or too much taxing—than when it was seen to be doing too little, e.g., that it should institute new or larger programs or provide more jobs. But again, the differences here were pretty small.

Table 6.7   Perceived Degree of Government Responsibility for Solving National Economic Problems, 1976 [a]

Most important national problem	Degree of responsibility			
	Great deal	Some	None	*n*
Inflation	82.4	16.1	1.5	461
Unemployment	75.4	23.6	0.9	533
Taxes	82.6	17.4	0.0	23
More government programs	82.4	15.7	2.0	51
Less government spending	91.2	8.8	0.0	34
General economic problems	78.6	19.4	1.9	206
Noneconomic problems	82.5	15.9	1.6	442
Total	79.9	18.6	1.5	1750

a. The government responsibility question was asked in reference to the problem respondents deemed most important. Thus this analysis could not be performed upon the most important national *economic* problem mentioned, which was used in the voting analysis, and so frequencies of the economic problem categories are slightly reduced.

Some of the apparent differences between the perceived levels of government responsibility for national versus personal problems undoubtedly result from differences in the wording of the questions. At the national level respondents were asked explicitly how responsible the government should be. At the personal level they were asked only "Who ought to be helping you with this?" But while not mentioning the government as a possibility might have made this question a very conservative indicator of perceived responsibility, many respondents who did cite the government probably considered its helping role to be very minor. It is also important to remember that the percentage of respondents who felt that the government should be doing something helpful was, in keeping with Sniderman and Brody's reasoning, quite high when the personal problem named was inflation or taxes. It seems safe to conclude, therefore, that almost all citizens hold those in power accountable for solving economic problems they believe affect the country as a whole. Unlike a wide range of personal economic problems, they cannot be seen as characteristic of one's own particular situation and thus dismissed as politically irrelevant.

Perceptions of Party Differences in Handling National Economic Problems

The analysis in the previous chapter went on to show, however, that the ethic of self-reliance was not the only factor which served to inhibit personal economic problems from influencing voting decisions. Another major factor was that voters often did not perceive any important differences between the major parties in their inclination or ability to help them with their most pressing personal problem. Data from the 1972 CPS study indicated that the only area in which respondents clearly favored one party over the other was unemployment. Over a quarter of those who cited unemployment or related problems believed that the Democrats were more likely to help them, while less than 3% of them felt assistance was more likely from the Republicans. Nineteen-seventy-two is the only year for which these data are available, so there is no way of knowing whether or not this pattern was present in other elections as well.

Given that the ethic of self-reliance has little relevance for what people see to be the most important national problems, perceptions of party differences are perhaps even more critical here than at the personal level. Second, the relationship between the evidence on voting and that on perceptions of party differences could take a number of different forms. Although voting in virtually every presidential election was significantly affected by perceptions of national economic problems, the particular problems which exerted these effects varied from one election to the next: the inflation-unemployment hypothesis dominated in 1960, 1976, and 1980, while the public sector hypothesis received its strongest support in 1964 and 1968. Perceptions of party differences may follow the same pattern, i.e., becoming quite large in some elections and disappearing entirely in others. Or perhaps the perceived merits and liabilities of the parties in different problem areas remain fairly constant from election to election. They inform voting when objective economic conditions, events, or candidates make different problems salient, but lie dormant, so to speak, when these problems do not occupy much of the electorate's attention.

The purpose here is not to disentangle beliefs concerning the ability of the parties to handle particular problems from more general partisan predispositions. Obviously the two are related—an individual who identifies with the Democratic party is going to be more likely than a nonidentifier to believe that the Democrats are better at handling a given problem. (What the analysis in chapter 5 showed, however, is that in many cases the groups of respondents who cited a particular personal economic problem did not, on the whole, believe one party was more likely to be helpful than the other.) Rather, the motive behind the analysis here is the same as before: to examine the results of the voting analysis in light of perceived party differences (or lack thereof) in handling different national problems.

Fortunately, it is not necessary, as it was in the respective analysis concerning personal economic problems, to rely upon evidence from only one study. In every presidential election year since 1960 respondents were asked, after they had named what they believed to be the most important national problems, which party was more likely to do what they wanted in regard to these problems.[23] A party difference index was computed for the economic concerns for which policy-oriented hypotheses were made (unemployment, inflation, taxes, more government programs, less government spending) by subtracting the percentage of respondents who thought that the Republicans would better handle the problem in question from the percentage who thought more highly of the Democrats. And, in order to have an indicator of how the public rated the overall problem-solving abilities of the parties from election to election, a party difference score was computed for *all* perceived national problems (economic and noneconomic) taken together.

Results of this arithmetic are reported in figure 6.2. Two clear patterns stand out. First, perceptions of the parties' abilities to handle national problems in general change considerably from

Figure 6.2
Perceptions of Party Differences in Handling
National Economic Problems, 1960-1980

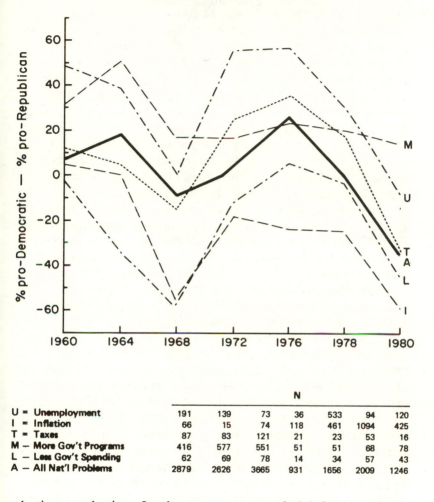

	N						
U = Unemployment	191	139	73	36	533	94	120
I = Inflation	66	15	74	118	461	1094	425
T = Taxes	87	83	121	21	23	53	16
M — More Gov't Programs	416	577	551	51	51	68	78
L — Less Gov't Spending	62	69	78	14	34	57	43
A — All Nat'l Problems	2879	2626	3665	931	1656	2009	1246

election to election. In the twenty-year period being examined
here, the trend has generally been an erosion of the perceived
prowess of the incumbent party. True, the standing of the Democrats relative to the Republicans was higher in 1964 than in 1960.
But during the next four years it slipped badly: by 1968, in fact,
more people believed the Republicans would deal better with
whatever national problem was of concern to them than would
the Democrats. Two Republican administrations later, however,

the percentage of people who named the Democrats as more likely "to get the government to do a better job" in dealing with national problems was again much higher than the percentage who named the Republicans. Moreover, the 1976 figure was much less an endorsement of the Democratic party than an indictment of the G.O.P.—less than 14% of the respondents polled in that year believed the national problem they deemed most important would be best handled by a Republican administration.

It follows that the Republicans' best hope for refurbishing their tarnished image was to have a Democrat back in the White House. Indeed, by the midterm election of 1978 the party differences index for all national problems favored the Democrats by just one point. Almost all of this change, though, represented Democratic slippage, not Republican gain: the percentage of respondents naming the Republicans as better able to handle what they perceived to be the nation's most serious problem rose to only 17%, while the percentage naming the Democrats dropped from 36% in 1976 to 18%. Over half the respondents in 1978, of course, believed that the nation's most pressing problem was inflation. Figures here were virtually identical to the overall figures: 16% felt inflation would be better handled by the Democrats, 20% believed the Republicans would do better, and 64% believed it made no difference which party was in power.

At this point, then, it appeared that the cycle of disaffection with first one party then the other as they moved in and out of office had been replaced by widespread exasperation over the perceived failure of both parties to come to grips with the nation's (primarily economic) problems. The findings of Alt's analysis indicate that the British electorate reacted in very much the same fashion to the ever-worsening performance of their nation's economy.[24] Alt and others have also argued that the failure of successive Labour and Conservative governments to reverse the trend of inflation and economic decline has resulted in an erosion of allegiances to both parties.[25] It is hard to take issue with this argument—there are probably few things as corrosive to party loyalties as the perception that neither party is more likely than the other to make any inroads against the country's most serious problems.

The next two years, however, persuaded a large portion of the populace that there really were differences in the major parties' problem-solving abilities. As in 1976, though, the figures in 1980 were much more an indictment of the incumbent party's record than an endorsement of their challengers. Only 11% of the respondents in the 1980 CPS surveys felt that the Democrats were better able to handle what they perceived to be the most important national problem, compared to 44% who instead favored the Republicans. Indeed, it is hard to find many bright spots in the second half of the Carter administration—the American public witnessed a rapid acceleration in the rate of inflation, a sharp increase in unemployment in the spring of 1980, historically high interest rates, and a collapse in housing and auto sales. In international affairs things were no better: the collapse of the Shah's regime and subsequent debacles in Iran, the Soviet invasion of Afghanistan, and the instability in Central America were only some of the troubles facing the United States abroad. It is hardly shocking to find, then, that few respondents in 1980 believed the Democrats were good for much of anything.

The second major feature of the evidence in figure 6.2, however, is that the ratings of the two parties have clearly and consistently varied over time across the different economic issue areas. In keeping with the policy-oriented hypotheses, the Democrats' standing relative to the Republicans was highest among respondents who cited unemployment, or who believed that new or larger federal programs were needed to address other serious national problems. Their standing vis-à-vis the Republicans was generally lower, on the other hand, among respondents who believed that the nation's worst problem was either inflation or too much government spending. And even though the number of respondents in the various categories changes tremendously from election to election, these differences persist across the entire twenty-year time period.

All in all, then, the findings in figure 6.2 parallel the findings of the voting analysis. People clearly react in an incumbency-oriented fashion to the record of the current officeholders, responding positively to success in the economic and other arenas but negatively to perceived failure. But they are also aware of differences in the parties' relative economic priorities, and consequently party ratings vary greatly across different problem areas. And as shown in the voting analysis (which took into account either past vote choices or partisan predispositions), in certain elections presidential candidates gain a significant measure of electoral support from voters who are concerned about the economic problems on which their party enjoys a comparative advantage.

Summary

The analyses undertaken in this chapter generated strong, consistent support for the national assessments version of the incumbency-oriented hypothesis. Voters' perceptions of recent trends in the nation's economy shifted dramatically in response to changes in the actual performance of the nation's economy. And the more favorable their assessments, the more likely they were to support candidates of the incumbent party. As was the case at the personal level, the influence of national economic assessments upon voting decisions was a good deal stronger in presidential elections than in congressional.

The findings of the analysis pertaining to perceived national economic problems compose a somewhat more complicated pattern, but one which endows substantial empirical backing—at least in presidential elections—to the policy-oriented versions of the national assessments hypothesis. The percentage of respondents in each survey who believed that either inflation or unemployment was the most serious problem facing the country closely paralleled the respective years' objective inflation and unemployment rates. The salience of the public sector issues, on the other hand, was highest during the prosperous decade of the 1960s. It appears that people view inflation, unemployment, or the general state of the economy as more pressing concerns, which, as the economy stumbled during the 1970s, took precedence over the question of whether the spending and taxing power of the government should be augmented or cut back.

Furthermore, each of the policy-oriented hypotheses fared best in those presidential election years in which large percentages of voters fell into the relevant categories. Thus the unemployment-inflation hypothesis received its strongest support in years in which one or both of these problems was severe enough to generate substantial public concern, i.e., 1960, 1976, and 1980. Similarly, voters' choices for president were most in line with the public sector hypothesis in 1964 and 1968. In contrast to the evidence at the presidential level, however, in the series of elections examined here voters' choices between the congressional candidates of the two major parties do not appear to have been consistently influenced by what they perceived to be the nation's most important economic problems.

As predicted, respondents believed the government bore a large degree of responsibility for handling whatever national problem they believed was most important. Unlike a wide variety of personal economic difficulties, problems deemed nationally troublesome could not be written off as peculiar to one's own circumstances or amenable to one's individual efforts. Finally, the data on perceived party differences were in broad agreement with the findings of the voting analyses. Although the public's confidence in the ability of the incumbent party to handle national problems in general usually declined during its tenure in office, there were large differences in the parties' standings relative to each other across different national economic problems. Respondents who cited unemployment as the major national economic concern, or who believed new or larger government programs were needed to address serious national problems, named the Democrats much more frequently than the Republicans as the party more capable of rectifying the situation. Ratings of the Republicans vis-à-vis the Democrats were much higher, on the other hand, among respondents who believed that the nation's worst problems were either inflation or excessive government spending.

7

Estimates of the Aggregate Effect of Personal Economic Experiences and National Economic Assessments upon Election Outcomes

This study has so far focused only upon the influence of economic concerns upon individual voters' decisions. At least part of the motivation for this and previous survey analyses in this area, however, comes from the evidence (generated by several time series analyses) of strong relationships between key economic indicators and the electoral fortunes of the incumbent party's presidential and congressional candidates. It is thus important to make some estimates of how much change in presidential and congressional election outcomes can be accounted for by the incumbency-oriented effects registered by the family finances and business conditions measures. The size of these cumulative effects, or course, depends not only upon how strongly these variables influence the decisions of individual voters, but also upon how much the distributions of these variables shift from election to election. Strong individual level effects may or may not add up to effects which are important in the aggregate. Conversely, it is quite possible for modest individual level effects to generate a substantial amount of change in the aggregate.

Estimates of the aggregate amount of interelection change which these two sets of measures could account for were obtained by means of the following simulation procedure. First, a probit estimate for each voter's behavior in a given presidential or congressional election was derived by multiplying that individual's values on each independent variable by the respective coefficient for each variable reported in tables 6.5 and 6.6 in the previous chapter. This probit estimate was then converted to a probability (of voting Republican) by evaluating that number on the cumulative standard normal distribution. These individual probability scores add up to the number of voters in the given election study who indicated that they voted Republican.

These calculations were then repeated after altering the values of the family finances variables (or business conditions variables) such that all voters were assigned the value of 0 in the "better" category and 1 in the "worse" category. This simulates the results of a given election had all voters behaved as if they were in the "worse" cateogry. Assuming that incumbency-oriented effects are operating in the correct direction, this procedure will result in simulated vote totals for the incumbent which are lower than the observed totals. Furthermore, the incumbents' simulated vote totals will be reduced by more in a good economic year than in a bad one, because a larger share of the voters in a bad year would be in the "worse" category to begin with. The difference between the decrements in the incumbents' share of the votes produced by this simulation in a good year and in a bad year, then, is an estimate of how much of the swing in the incumbents' electoral support is due to these variables.

A potential problem facing this simulation is the bias which could be introduced by a great deal of asymmetry between the size of the estimates of a pair of "better" or "worse" terms. This is because the shift in the simulated behavior of voters in the "same" category (i.e., to vote as if they were in the "worse" category) would be inordinately large or inordinately small. To be sure, if one of the two terms was systematically larger in absolute value across the entire series of elections, e.g., if voters punished the incumbent with greater fervor for things being worse, we would naturally want to retain this asymmetry of effects in this simulation. As noted earlier, however, this was not the case: estimates of the "worse" terms were not on average larger than those of the "better" terms, or vice versa. Representative good and bad years for this simulation should thus be chosen so as to minimize this source of potential bias.

The years picked to make interelection comparisons at the presidential level were 1972 and 1980. The main thing the 1972 election has going for it, of course, is that it was one of the most prosperous years in the series. Fortunately, it is also the case that the differences between estimates of the family finances and national business conditions "better" and "worse" terms (.35 and .51, respectively), were quite close to the averages for the entire series. On the other hand, 1980 was the worst year (economically speaking) for which both sets of measures were available. In the equation for that year the differences between the family finances and business conditions "better" and "worse" terms were virtually identical to series averages of .28 and .47, respectively.

To be sure, there is a substantial degree of asymmetry between the size of 1980 business conditions estimates, i.e., the "worse" term is .33, the "better" term only -.14. The potential problem of bias discussed earlier is minimized, however, by the very small size of the "same" category (less than 15% of the voters). The major remaining problem of this nature is with the family finances estimates in the 1972 presidential election: the "worse" term is much larger (in absolute value) than the "better" term, implying that the size of the decrement in the incumbent's vote share resulting from this simulation will be inordinately large. The other advantages of the 1972 presidential equation, however, indicate that it is best to use it anyway and simply remain mindful of this potential problem.

The results of these calculations revealed that shifting all voters into the family finances "worse" category would have "cost" the incumbent presidential candidates nearly 4% more of the vote in 1972 than in 1980. This is a sizeable difference (because of the problems with the 1972 family finances terms discussed earlier, this figure might also be a slight overestimate). However, shifting all voters into the national business conditions "worse" category would have cost the incumbent nearly 7% more in 1972 than in 1980. Voters' perceptions of recent trends in the nation's economy clearly account for considerably more electoral change than do their judgments about how they and their families have fared financially. The point should be made again, though, that the greater aggregate effects of general assessments of the nation's economy do not derive solely from the somewhat stronger influence this variable has upon individual voters' decisions. It is also the case (as shown in figure 6.1) that these assessments shift much more dramatically from a relatively prosperous year like 1972 to an economically troubled year like 1980 than do their judgments about how well or poorly they themselves fared economically. It is as a consequence of both factors that national economic assessments account for considerably more change in the outcomes of presidential elections.

Now this hardly implies that the aggregate effects associated with personal economic conditions are unimportant. Presidential candidates typically lose sleep over much smaller numbers of votes. Assessments of personal and national economic conditions, furthermore, both respond in the same direction to objective economic change. In this case, their joint effects produced an 11% swing against the incumbent between these two years. Or, put another way, the increase in the number of voters who believed that either they themselves or the nation as a whole was in worse shape economically than a year ago accounted for about a third of the difference between the incumbent president's landslide victory in 1972 and his bruising defeat in 1980.

This simulation was repeated at the congressional level, but the 1962 and 1980 equations were used for comparisons. Nineteen-sixty-two was chosen as the test case for good years because the effects associated with both pairs of "better" and "worse" terms were about equal in magnitude, and because the differences between them (.10 for the family finances terms, .36 for the national business conditions terms) were pretty close to the series average. Differences between these pairs of estimates in 1980 were also very close to the series average. As in the presidential election equation, any bias resulting from the large degree of asymmetry between the business conditions "better" and "worse" terms is mitigated by the small size of the "same" category.

A drawback in using these years is the fact that voters' economic assessments were not as favorable in 1962 as they were in other years (e.g., 1964), nor were they quite as unfavorable in 1980 as in 1974. Unfortunately, the requisite data are not available for these other years. The range over which the distribution of the two variables shifted in this time period, then, was actually somewhat greater than the range between 1962 and 1980; consequently, this procedure will probably slightly underestimate the amount of change in congressional election outcomes accounted for by the family finances and national business conditions measures.

At any rate, shifting all voters into the "worse" categories of these two variables lowered the incumbent party's vote total 3.5% more in 1962 than in 1980. Virtually all of this difference was associated with the national business conditions items. As at the presidential level, then, voters' perceptions of trends in the nation's economy had a much stronger effect upon election outcomes than judgments as to how they themselves had been faring economically.

The joint effect of these variables—a 3.5% swing in the incumbent party's vote totals between 1962 and 1980—is probably somewhat less than it was between the more extreme years of 1964 and 1974. Still, it is surely the case that the incumbency-oriented effects of these variables produce much less interelection change at the congressional level than at the presidential. It is also true, though, that there is much less variance in the congressional election series during this time period: Democrats won a majority of votes in every election, their share of the two-party total ranging between 50.8% in 1968 to 59.6% in 1974. Thus a loss of 3.5% by the incumbents between a pretty good year and a pretty bad year is a large proportion of the swings actually observed in this time series, e.g., the 5.2% drop suffered by the incumbent Republicans between 1956 and 1958. In short, even though the absolute magnitude of the aggregate, incumbency-oriented effects of these economic variables is smaller at the congressional level than at the presidential, these effects account for a larger share of the total swing in congressional election outcomes than in presidential election outcomes.

The next comparisons to be made are between the cumulative electoral effects of personally experienced economic problems and those of perceived national economic problems. In presidential elections, first of all, estimates of the head of household unemployment terms were generally more pro-Democratic, compared to their respective reference groups, than the estimates of the national unemployment terms. In 1972 and 1976, of course, it is possible to compare differences in the estimates of the personal level inflation and unemployment terms with differences at the national level. Although the inflation-unemployment difference was somewhat larger at the national level in 1976, in 1972 the difference was quite large at the personal level and non-existent at the national level. Moreover, at the congressional level the economic problems voters perceived to be nationally most important rarely appeared to influence their choices between the major parties' candidates. For any one individual, it appears that being personally affected by unemployment or finding inflation personally troublesome has a somewhat larger impact upon his or her choice for president than simply perceiving unemployment or inflation to be a serious national problem.

But as shown in the previous chapter, in the years in which comparisons are possible (1972-76), the number of voters who felt inflation or unemployment was nationally troublesome was much larger than the number of those who reported either to be their most important personal problem. This is especially true of unemployment: in 1976, for instance, 32% cited it at the national level, compared to 4% at the personal. This means that in years of relatively high unemployment or high inflation, the cross-sectional effects of these economic issues upon presidential elections stem much more from voters who see them as pressing national problems than from voters who find them personally troublesome.

What we have just discussed here, of course, are cross-sectional effects, which exert either a pro-Democratic or Pro-Republican influence over different groups of voters in a given election. The final task to be taken up is to estimate how much change in election outcomes can be accounted for by shifts in the distribution of public concern over unemployment vis-à-vis inflation. As was shown earlier, changing macroeconomic circumstances provoke much larger shifts in perceptions of national economic problems than in the problems people report as personally most bothersome. Indeed, in the two presidential election years for which the personal problem data are available (1972 and 1976), the percentages of respondents who cited a given personal economic problem were nearly identical. The following analysis will thus be confined to national problems only.

Inspection of table 6:1 indicates that one of the most unfavorable swings (from the incumbent president's point of view) in public concern over unemployment vis-à-vis inflation occurred between 1976, when both problems were highly salient, and 1980, when concern over inflation was clearly dominant. Most of this shift, of course, can be characterized as a decline in the saliency of unemployment. Furthermore, estimates of the national unemployment terms were quite similar: -.40 in 1976 and -.50 in 1980. A good estimate of how much change in the outcomes of these two elections resulted from this shift in the public's macro-economic priorities can thus be obtained by setting the effects of the national unemployment dummies at zero in both years and comparing the changes in vote totals.

These calculations reveal that the decline in the salience of unemployment vis-à-vis inflation produced a 1.2% shift against Carter from 1976 to 1980. This erosion in support is nontrivial. On the other hand, the earlier analysis of interelection change due to incumbency-oriented voting indicates that this is not nearly as much slippage as that which resulted from the unfavorable shift in general assessments of national business conditions. It appears, then, that incumbency-oriented votes against Carter in response to the overall poorer performance of the economy played a much larger role in his demise than did the votes he lost as result of the shift in public concern away from the traditionally pro-Democratic issue of unemployment to the traditionally pro-Republican issue of inflation.

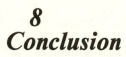

8
Conclusion

This study of the effects of economic concerns upon voters' decisions in American elections has revolved around two central questions. First, is voting incumbency-oriented or policy-oriented? Second, do voters respond to economic problems they have personally experienced, or to their perceptions of economic conditions in the nation as a whole? For someone looking for simple yes-no answers, the results of this intensive examination of these questions are probably not very satisfying; indeed, the voting analyses have generated at least some evidence in support of both the personal experiences and national assessments versions of both the incumbency-oriented and policy-oriented hypotheses. Nevertheless, a number of broad patterns have repeatedly emerged from the data. A good way to conclude, then, is to identify these patterns and to discuss the implications they have for theory and research on voting and electoral competition.

Presidential Elections and Congressional Elections

First of all, no matter what particular hypothesis was being tested, evidence in support of it was virtually always stronger in presidential elections than in congressional. This is hardly surprising, of course—the president's role in the economic arena is preeminent. It is the president who is primarily responsible for the general thrust of macroeconomic policy, whether it be the "guns and butter" policies of Lyndon Johnson or the "Reaganomics" of the current administration. It is also the president who shoulders most of the credit or blame for the ultimate success or failure of the policies pursued by his administration. Consequently, any sort of economic problem which voters might be concerned about will exert a larger influence upon their choice between presidential candidates than upon that between the candidates for Congress.

This difference between presidential and congressional elections, of course, is not confined to economic matters. Decades of public opinion research have shown that the president occupies a central place in the public's mind—virtually all Americans know who the president is, which party he belongs to, his general ideological orientation, and have formed fairly firm positive or negative evaluations of him. In contrast, voters' knowledge of the candidates running for Congress in their district is usually pretty sketchy. To be sure, the findings of Mann and Wolfinger's study indicate that congressional candidates are not the invisible men and women earlier research had suggested they were.[1] Public awareness of the president, though, is much much greater.

Another factor which probably contributed to the greater empirical support which the various hypotheses garnered at the presidential level is the simple fact that all voters were choosing between the same candidates. The congressional equations, on the other hand, utilized data on voters participating in several dozen different elections. Each one of these elections, of course, was contested by a unique pair of candidates in a unique set of circumstances. As Kinder and Kiewiet put it, each congressional election "reflects a special mix of factors: idiosyncratic factors, particular and sometimes peculiar local conditions, diversity in the 'home style' chosen by the incumbent, and so forth. . . . But thanks to nationwide news networks, presidential campaigns are much more homogeneous, being roughly the same in Peoria as in Los Angeles."[2] There is, then, a large, nonsystematic component to voters' choices between local congressional candidates which generally does not influence their voting for president.

That the dependent variables in the congressional equations reflected the choices offered in dozens of different campaigns would seem to be an especially important factor in accounting for the major discrepancy between the findings at the presidential versus the congressional level—although the national assessments policy-oriented hypotheses received strong support in the former set of elections, they received little empirical backing in the latter. This pattern of evidence is, to an important extent, likely due to the fact that there is a great deal of ideological dispersion in both major parties' contingents of congressional candidates. Large numbers of Democrats running for Congress have no trouble reconciling their party membership with a thoroughgoing conservatism in economic affairs. Their colleagues across the aisle also differ a great deal in their tolerance of federal government activity and in the zeal of their inflation-fighting. Now this is not to say there are no central tendencies in the major parties' ideologies and macroeconomic priorities. There are. But it is also undoubtedly true that in many congressional elections these traditional party differences are not expressed with any real clarity.

Of all the local, "contextual" factors operating in congressional elections, however, probably none are more important than the overall quality of the candidates and their ability to raise campaign funds.[3] Taking this into consideration, Fiorina reasoned that these variables are themselves affected by national economic conditions, and thus constitute an important if indirect route by which the state of the economy can influence congressional election outcomes. As he put it:

> Perhaps election returns vary not with objective economic conditions but with self-fulfilling expectations about those conditions held by the candidates and parties. Take 1974, for example. Everyone expects a Republican disaster. Thus, serious Republican candidates wait for a more propitious time before seeking office (or a move to a higher office), and Republican incumbents find voluntary retirement more attractive than usual. Meanwhile Republican contributors hesitate to invest funds in an apparently lost cause. Thus, the Republican ticket is composed of underfinanced cannon fodder. In contrast, the Democrats have a plenitude of enthusiastic candidates lavishly financed by those who know a good investment when they see one. Does the

Republican decline at the polls reflect objective economic conditions? Or does it reflect a combination of poorer than usual, underfinanced Republican candidates, and better than usual, adequately financed Democratic ones? [4]

In other words, the strong aggregate level relationships between economic conditions and congressional election outcomes are far less a product of voters' reactions to economic conditions than of parties', candidates', and campaign contributors' self-fulfilling expectations about their reactions.

A recent study by Jacobson and Kernell amassed a substantial body of evidence supporting these conjectures.[5] Compared to their counterparts in 1972 or 1976, Republicans challenging incumbent Democratic congressmen in 1974 raised and spent much less campaign money. They were also considerably less likely to have held previous elective office. Neither Fiorina nor Jacobson and Kernell claim, of course, that the self-fulfilling expectations of potential candidates and contributors are the entire story. If it were true that voters responded only to the relative quality of congressional candidates and their campaigns, experienced, well-financed Republican candidates would have done just as well in 1974 as in 1972, and Republican losses in 1974 would have been entirely self-inflicted. Presumably this would not happen very many times before politicians, who are not in the business of getting these things wrong, would discover that such strategies were badly flawed.

The results of the congressional voting analyses reported in chapter 6, however, strongly indicate that elites need not worry about whether or not the electorate is a paper tiger. It is not. Individual voters do react to the state of the economy when choosing between congressional candidates. Although the national assessments policy-oriented hypotheses met with little success at the congressional level, the national assessments version of the incumbency-oriented hypothesis won strong support: the more unfavorably voters evaluated recent trends in national business conditions, the more likely they were to oppose candidates of the incumbent president's party. There is, as noted earlier, a great deal of ideological dispersion in the policy preferences of the parties' congressional candidates. When it comes to voters' general assessments of the performance of the economy, however, they are seen, to some extent, as members of alternative governing teams. And when they belong to the party of the incumbent president, they share at least some of the electoral blame for a slumping economy and part of the credit for prosperity.

Moreover, the findings of the previous chapter also indicated that changes in voters' assessments of the national economy account for a large proportion of the total swing in the incumbent party's vote totals from good years to bad. Now this is not to say that the electoral consequences of elites' anticipated reactions are unimportant. Republican candidates in 1974, for example, clearly were less experienced and less well bankrolled than in other years, and this had to have a deleterious effect on their performance at the polls. What should be stressed, though, is that the reaction of voters to economic conditions which are being anticipated by potential candidates and contributors are very real, and are electorally very important.[6]

Personal Economic Experiences and National Economic Assessments

One of the basic lines of inquiry in this study concerned the degree to which voters' decisions were influenced by two different types of economic information: their own personal encounters with economic problems and conditions in the nation's economy. As indicated earlier, the findings of the voting analyses did not line up entirely behind one hypothesis or the other. There was instead solid evidence of voters responding to both types of information. The main reason why individuals would be inclined to consider personally encountered economic conditions in deciding how to vote, obviously, is that this sort of information is so immediate and so tangible; these experiences are, as Fiorina, puts it, particularly hard pieces of data. Moreover, Adam Smith's characterization of human nature—"Every man feels his own pleasures and his own pains more sensibly than those of other people"—would appear to remain at least a good first approximation. There is a certain poignancy about receiving a pink slip which cannot be conveyed by a news story that unemployment rose .3% in the previous month.

There are, on the other hand, important factors which act to deflect the impact of personal economic experiences upon voting decisions. In general, Americans tend to attribute their own economic fortunes to forces which are not directly related to national economic trends or to the government's macroeconomic policies. The data also evince an enduring commitment to the ethic of self-reliance. When asked in the 1972 CPS election study who, if anybody, should be helping them with their most serious personal problems, only a small minority of respondents referred to the government in general or to a particular public agency. Instead, most felt that they themselves were primarily responsible for dealing with their problems as best they could.

Conditions in the nation's economy, of course, are probably not as personally salient to most individuals as their own financial situation. But national economic assessments are, by definition, of general, widespread phenomena. Consequently, in most people's minds national economic conditions reflect upon the performance and policies of the incumbent administration much more directly than the conditions of their own lives. The data in table 6.7 provide very strong evidence on this point; regardless of the particular problem respondents believed was the most important for the nation, the vast majority felt the government bore a great deal of responsibility for solving it. In short, what national economic assessments lack in personal relevance, they make up for by being of more obvious political relevance.

To be sure, the degree to which people believed that they themselves were primarily responsible for coping with their personal economic problems varied significantly. In particular, a very large majority of those whose most serious personal problem was inflation indicated that the government should be trying to curb it. This is undoubtedly due to the nature of inflation itself. When people see food, fuel, or housing prices rising they know that prices are rising not just for themselves, but for everybody. Unlike their encounters with a wide variety of other economic problems, people understand that the inflation they themselves observe is symptomatic of a problem affecting the entire economy, and that there is little they, as individuals, can do about it. The combination of personal relevance and perceived universality undoubtedly makes the potential impact of inflation upon voters' choices especially strong.

In general, though, the strong points of one type of economic information tend to complement the shortcomings of the other. It is thus quite reasonable for voters to take both personal experiences and national assessments into account. Of the two, however, it is national assessments which have the greater electoral consequences. Estimates of the incumbency-oriented effect associated with the national business conditions measures were generally larger than respective estimates of the family finances terms. But more importantly, objective changes in the performance of the economy cause much larger shifts in the distribution of the national business conditions variable. As a consequence, changing perceptions of the national economy account for a considerably larger proportion of the swing in support for the incumbent party from good years to bad than do changes in personal economic conditions. A similar situation obtains with policy-oriented voting. If anything, for any one individual, being personally affected by unemployment or finding inflation to be personally troublesome tended to exert a larger influence upon voting than did simply perceiving inflation or unemployment to be a serious national problem. In years in which inflation or unemployment is running at a fairly high level, though, the proportion of voters who believe these are serious national problems is much larger than the proportion of voters who find these problems personally troublesome. It is thus the national problem perceptions which have the larger cumulative electoral effects.

As was pointed out in chapter 2, voting in response to national economic assessments could reflect very different motivations. It could have its basis in a purely patriotic or altruistic concern for the interests of all Americans. Alternatively, it could be entirely motivated by a self-interested concern for one's own economic well-being; in this case voters simply use information about national economic conditions as an indicator of how well the incumbent administration has promoted their own (and their fellow citizens') welfare. For this reason the distinction between the personal experiences and national assessments hypotheses was properly characterized as informational, not motivational.

Of course one might attempt to assess voters' motivations, but this would seem to be a task for which conventional survey methods are particularly ill-suited—answers to questions such as "Do you vote on the basis of what is good for you personally or what is good for the country?" would have to be taken with more than a grain of salt. Furthermore, concern over whether the influence of national assessments upon voting decisions grows out of a regard for one's own interest or the national interest may be largely misplaced. The more important point is that in most voters' minds the two motives are most probably not in conflict, but are instead congruent and reinforcing. To be sure, the evidence in this and in other studies indicates that for most people most of the time the connection between national trends and governmental policies and their own economics is a tenuous one. They frequently report that while they themselves are doing well, national business conditions are on the skids—or vice versa. Different sectors of the economy, of course, vary a great deal in the degree to which their fortunes rise and fall with trends in national business conditions. And there are a few businesses which are countercyclical, e.g., mortgage foreclosure or repossession services.

Still, it seems likely that most people would accept the premise that, *ceteris paribus*, they themselves would probably be in better shape economically when the national economy performs well than when it performs poorly. That voters value national prosperity, which they clearly do, implies that they would rather live in a world in which economic well-being is increasing and economic opportunities are expanding—for themselves and for everybody else. Concern over one's personal interest and the national interest thus run in the same direction, resulting in what de Tocqueville referred to as an "enlightened" sense of self-interest. Enlightened self-interest, de Tocqueville believed, was the real basis for the success of American democracy. As he put it:

> There is another sort of patriotism more rational than that; less generous, perhaps less ardent, but more creative and more lasting, it is engendered by enlightenment, grown by the aid of laws and the exercise of rights, and in the end becomes, in a sense, mingled with personal interest. A man understands the influence which his country's well-being has on his own; he knows the law allows him to contribute to the production of this well-being, and he takes an interest in his country's prosperity, first as a thing useful to him and then as something he has created.[7]

Incumbency-oriented and Policy-oriented Voting

To a large extent, survey researchers' interest in this area of inquiry was sparked by the observed aggregate level relationships between economic conditions and national election outcomes which time series analyses by Kramer and others had documented. It should be realized, though, that there are so many differences between the two types of studies that it is simply not possible to determine with available survey data the exact mix of microlevel factors which yield the macrolevel relationships. First, there is only a very rough correspondence between the aggregate objective measures used in the time series studies and the individual perceptions and evaluations of economic conditions which constitute the independent variables in survey analyses. Second, the time periods examined are typically very different: Kramer's analysis, for example, began with the 1896 election. This was not only decades before the advent of survey research, but also antedated television, national news networks, and the monthly roll call of inflation, unemployment, industrial production, and other national economic statistics. There is every reason to suspect that had the survey data analyzed in this study been available for 1904, 1928, or even 1946, the results might have been very different. Third, the behavior examined in this and most other survey analyses—the choices made by those individuals who participated in a given election—is only one of several important factors which are affected by economic conditions and which in turn affect aggregate vote totals. The decisions of incumbent congressmen to retire or not, of potential candidates to run or not, and of voters to turn out or not are only a few examples of such factors.[8] It is thus much more accurate to characterize survey analyses in this area as attempts to find individual level relationships which *are consistent with* the aggregate level findings.

The attempts made in this study were quite successful. Consistent with the findings of several time series analyses, which showed that the electoral fortunes of the incumbent president and congressional candidates of his party rise and fall with short-term economic fluctuations, the analyses undertaken here generated strong evidence of incumbency-oriented voting at the individual level. The more favorably voters assessed recent trends in the nation's economy and in their own financial situation, the more likely they were to support the incumbents. In general, the economic variables which registered the strongest effects upon aggregate vote totals were measures of change in per capita income.[9] The reason for this is almost surely not that it is the income change statistics which are most salient to voters. Few voters have probably ever heard of or have more than a vague notion of what "per capita GNP" might mean. Rather, it is probably the case that it is these indicators which are most highly correlated with the simple, retrospective evaluations which exert a clear, consistent influence upon voters' choices from one election to the next. Kinder and Kiewiet reported that for the 1956-76 period the correlation (Pearson r) between the average of responses to the family finances question and change in per capita disposable real income was .68.[10] Similarly, for the period beginning in 1960 the correlation between the mean of responses to the national business conditions question and change in per capita real GNP was .91. In contrast, correlations between these survey measures and the unemployment rate, the inflation rate, and the often touted "misery index" (the sum of the inflation and unemployment rates) were considerably lower.

This study was also successful in generating evidence in favor of the inflation-unemployment policy-oriented hypothesis. In those years in which large portions of the electorate believed the nation's most serious economic problem was either inflation or unemployment, voters who were concerned about the former problem were much more likely to support the Republican candidate for president than were voters worried about the latter problem. In the few years in which the data were available (1972-76) it appeared that voters who found inflation to be their most important personal economic problem also voted Republican more often than did individuals whose most serious problem was unemployment-related. Data on head of household unemployment, of course, were present in virtually every election year. With few exceptions, voters whose family head was currently or had been out of work gave greater than average support to Democratic candidates.

As noted in chapter 2, a couple of aggregate level time series analyses had also found that high levels of unemployment tended to be associated with greater support for Democratic candidates; unlike the present study, however, they did not find a pro-Republican effect associated with inflation.[11] There are many reasons why the aggregate level studies might not have picked up effects of this nature. Probably the most important, though, is that the chronic year-in, year-out inflation which has troubled the economy during the past few decades is a recent phenomenon. Although sharp bursts of inflation did occur after the World

Wars, it was not until the postwar period that the general price level began to climb steadily upward—seven of the national elections between 1896 and 1938, in fact, occurred in years of falling prices. Furthermore, rising prices were usually associated with periods of prosperity and falling prices with periods of depression. In short, the price level series in the first half of this century behaved very differently than it has in the second half, and voters' reaction to rising prices may have been very different. It is thus not too surprising that analyses of time series data extending back several decades have usually not found consistent electoral effects associated with changes in prices.

It should also be remembered that inflation is not simply the flip side of unemployment. Although reducing these problems poses conflicting macroeconomic goals, inflation and unemployment vary considerably along a number of dimensions. Perhaps the most important difference is in the nature of the costs they inflict. Although the psychological costs should not be underestimated, the objective economic costs of unemployment are substantial. The major costs associated with inflation, on the other hand, are not objective income and wealth effects, but rather the more intangible (though very real) costs of living in a more uncertain world. Another major difference is in the way the costs of inflation and unemployment are distributed. There were large differences across racial, occupational, and age groups in the percentage of respondents who named unemployment their most serious economic problem—differences which paralleled the objective rates of unemployment in these groups. The impact of inflation, though, appeared to be spread much more evenly across the population. The propensity of respondents to name inflation their worst economic problem bore virtually no relationship to the particular age, income, or occupational group to which they belonged, or to their level of educational attainment. This finding is consistent with most economic analyses of the costs and benefits of inflation. As Piachaud puts it, "inflation acts neither as Robin Hood nor as Robber Baron; neither the poor nor the rich are affected in a uniform way."[12] In terms of its costs and the distribution of its costs, then, unemployment lines up neatly with the lines of cleavage which were drawn at the time of the New Deal. Inflation does not.

This would seem to suggest that aversion to inflation might constitute a "cross-cutting" cleavage which would further weaken the already tenuous socioeconomic basis of the current party system. But this is probably not the case because the methods generally used to combat inflation—restrictive monetary and/or fiscal policies—result, at least in the short run, in a reduction in real economic activity, employment, and income. The costs entailed by such a slowdown, of course, are borne disproportionately by different occupational, racial, and age groups, i.e. in a manner congruent with current party divisions. So although aversion to inflation is distributed roughly equally across major demographic and socioeconomic groups, aversion to the side effects of anti-inflation therapy is not. And finally, the findings of the voting analyses and the analysis of party perceptions (see figure 6.2) clearly demonstrate that inflation is a relatively pro-Republican issue, and does not tend to cut across existing partisan lines.

There emerged from this study, then, a substantial amount of evidence in support of both the incumbency-oriented and policy-oriented hypotheses. Again, however, one might ask which is more important. If one were forced to analyze American national elections in terms of only one of these two hypotheses, which one would it be?

For a couple of reasons, the more important of the political consequences of economic concerns are the incumbency-oriented ones. As mentioned earlier, the poorest showing of any of the various hypotheses was turned in by the national assessments, policy-oriented hypotheses in the congressional election equations. In contrast, voters' general assessments of the nation's economy clearly influenced the degree to which they supported congressional candidates of the incumbent president's party. Futhermore, results of the voting simulations strongly indicated that it was voters' incumbency-oriented reactions to their family's financial situation and to their general assessments of the economy which accounted for the lion's share of the shifts in the incumbent president's share of the vote from election to election.

An incumbent president, of course, may not find these results to be a particularly helpful guide to action—any more, say, than stating, "To get reelected, make sure your policies are successful." It is possible, though, to cast this advice to the current administration more precisely—i.e., get inflation down without running up an unacceptably high rate of unemployment. As table 6.1 shows, inflation has been the public's dominant economic concern for the past decade. Inflation continues to be cited by a large percentage of survey respondents as a serious national problem. In the years in which the data were available (1972-76) the percentage of Americans who felt inflation was their worst personal economic problem far exceeded the percentage of individuals who cited unemployment. It seems certain that the American public is and will continue to be keenly interested in the success or failure of those in power to come to grips with this problem.

As of this writing it is clear that the Reagan administration has enjoyed a substantial degree of success in reducing the rate of inflation, but the level of unemployment is higher than at any time since the Great Depression. What the key political question is, then, is equally clear: Just how unacceptable is this high rate of joblessness? At this point there is substantial reason to believe that the downside political risks of unemployment to the current administration are a good deal smaller than a proemployment advocate would like. As indicated earlier, a swing in public concern away from the traditionally pro-Republican issue of inflation to the traditionally pro-Democratic issue of unemployment is probably not in and of itself all that damaging. Far more important politically is the voters' general sense of whether the nation's economy is, on the whole, getting better or getting worse. The findings of Hibbs's analysis of public opinion data from 1971 through 1976 present a similar picture. As Hibbs characterized his results, "at all *stable* unemployment rates a solid majority of the public is likely to be more averse to inflation than unemployment *if* the rate of inflation runs higher than 6 percent per annum."[13]

After five additional years of chronic inflation, it may well be that the public's tolerance of high unemployment for the sake of reducing inflation may now be even greater than Hibbs's findings indicated. The outcome of the 1982 midterm elections—a Republican loss of twenty-six seats in the House and none in the Senate—certainly does not add up to the Republican disaster which consideration of the unemployment rate alone would have presaged. If in a few years from now the nation's economy appears to be moving in a generally favorable direction, the current administration could survive a rate of unemployment which, by historical standards anyway, is very high.

Appendix 1
Probit Analysis

The most commonly used multivariate statistical model in the social sciences is ordinary least squares (OLS) regression. This technique is inappropriate for the analyses of voting undertaken in this study, however, because of problems arising from the dichotomous nature of the dependent variables. Although this variable can best be characterized as the probability of voting one way or another, the only observed values are 0 (voting Republican, say) and 1 (voting Democratic). Given that this is the case, a key assumption of the OLS model—constant variance of the error term across all observations—is violated.

The statistical model underlying probit analysis removes this problem by assuming that the relationship between the independent variables and the probabilistic dependent variable is not linear (as OLS assumes), but follows instead the S-shaped cumulative normal distribution. The differences between these two models is displayed in figure A.1, which is taken from a study by Aldrich and Cnudde.[1]

As is shown clearly in figure A.1, one of the worst pathologies of using OLS on a dichotomous dependent variable is that predicted values can exceed 1 or be less than 0. The nonlinear probit model is obviously free of this problem. As a consequence of the

Figure A.1: Comparison of the Probit and OLS Models
(1972 presidential election data)

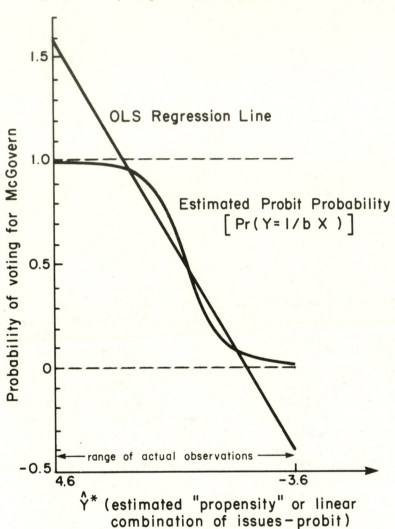

nonlinearity, however, probit estimates cannot be interpreted in the same way as OLS regression coefficients, which indicate the amount of change in the dependent variable produced by a unit change in the independent variable. A linear estimate holds across the entire distribution. A coefficient of .1, for example, would mean a unit increase in that variable would move one respondent from a .80 to a .90 probability of voting Republican, or another from .40 to .50. A probit estimate, in contrast, indicates movements along the cumulative normal distribution. A probit estimate of .20, for example, would mean a unit increase in that variable would move one respondent from a .50 to a .58 probability of voting Republican, but another respondent would be moved only from a .90 to a .93 probability.

For a thorough treatment of probit analysis see Finney.[2] Most econometrics textbooks also discuss this technique. Aldrich and Cnudde, besides comparing the results of a probit analysis with those obtained from OLS, also report comparisons with estimates derived from discriminant analysis.[3]

Appendix 2
Construction of Social
Background Variables

As discussed in chapter 3, Cross-sectional Model 3 specifies a battery of socioeconomic and demographic variables as predictors of voting behavior in national elections. A few of the election studies lacked data on one or two of the variables, and in a few others one or two variables were operationalized in slightly different ways. In almost all cases, though, the variables were constructed as follows:

Family income. A nine-point ordinal scale. Because of a steady rise in average income and inflation, the actual dollar amounts signified by each category rose from election to election. In 1956, for example, the highest category was for all incomes over $10,000 per year, while in 1978 it required an annual income of over $35,000 to make the top bracket. Every attempt was made, however, to make the percentage totals in each category as balanced as possible.

Educational attainment. An eight-point ordinal scale. As with income, the average level of education in the United States rose steadily during this time period. As before, the categories were defined to yield as even a distribution of frequencies as possible.

Birth cohort. Two dummy variables, one for voters who entered the electorate prior to the Great Depression, another for voters who became eligible to vote for the first time between 1932 and 1944.

Race. A dummy variable, taking on the value of 1 if the respondent was black, 0 otherwise.

Religion. Two dummy variables, one for Catholic voters, one for Jewish voters, with Protestants being the reference group.

Occupation. A series of dummy variables. Wherever possible the general categories of the Political Behavior Occupational Code were used, with respondents not belonging to the labor force being the reference group. Dummies were specified for business-professional people, owners and managers of retail establishments, clerical and sales personnel, skilled workers, unskilled workers, service workers, and for farmers.

Union membership. A dummy variable indicated whether or not anyone in the respondent's household belonged to a union.

Region of residence. Three dummy variables, one for the South, one for the West, and for Midwest. Respondents from the Northeast and Mid-Atlantic States made up the reference group.

Appendix 3

Table A.1 1976 Presidential Election: Five Alternative Specifications

Variable	1972 vote	1974 party identification	1974 party id. instrument
Constant	.25/(.19)	.34/(.19)*	.57/(.16)
Republican	.67/(.13)**	.62/(.15)**	—
Democrat	-.73/(.15)**	-.88/(.14**	-1.10/(.11)**
Personal economic experiences			
Family finances better	-.02/(.11)	-.07/(.11)	-.05/(.11)
Family finances worse	-.19/(.12)	-.14/(.12)	-.15/(.12)
Inflation	-.01/(.12)	.02/(.12)	.03/(.12)
Declining real income	-.01/(.21)	-.08/(.21)	-.16/(.20)
Unemployment	-.24/(.27)	-.30/(.27)	-.09/(.26)
Taxes	.02/(.23)	-.06/(.24)	.17/(.23)
General economic problems	-.08/(.13)	-.11/(.13)	-.11/(.12)
National economic assessments			
Business conditions better	.53/(.11)**	.49/(.12)**	.52/(.11)**
Business conditions worse	-.15/(.13)	-.13/(.13)	-.23/(.13)
Unemployment	-.40/(.15)**	-.50/(.16)**	-.52/(.15)**
Inflation	.08/(.15	-.01/(.16)	-.05/(.15)
Taxes	-.04/(.41)	-.08/(.40)	-.27/(.40)
More government programs	.15/(.27)	.07/(.28)	-.07/(.26)
Less government spending	.22/(.34)	.15/(.38)	.31/(.34)
General economic problems	-.03/(.17)	-.25/(.18)	-.21/(.17)
$\hat{R}^2$	.40	.44	.36
n	923	923	923

* $p < .05$ ** $p < .01$

Table A.1   1976 Presidential Election: Five Alternative Specifications *(cont.)*

Variable	1976 party identification	1976 socioeconomic background variables
Constant	.36/(.21	.01/(.23)
Republican	.97/(.17)**	—
Democrat	-1.06/(.15)**	—
Personal economic experiences		
Family finances better	.04/(.12)	-.00/(.11)
Family finances worse	-.09/(.13)	-.10/(.12)
Inflation	.09/(.13)	.05/(.12)
Declining real income	-.00/(.22)	-.21/(.20)
Unemployment	-.11/(.29)	-.01/(.27)
Taxes	-.29/(.25)	.12/(.23)
General economic problems	-.02/(.14)	-.12/(.13)
National economic assessments		
Business conditions better	.33/(.13)**	.48/(.12)**
Business conditions worse	-.21/(.14)	-.24/(.13)*
Unemployment	-.50/(.17)**	-.56/(.15)**
Inflation	-.09/(.17)	.06/(.15)
Taxes	.08/(.41)	-.19/(.41)
More government programs	-.25/(.30)	-.06/(.27)
Less government spending	.18/(.42)	.28/(.34)
General economic problems	-.43/(.20)**	-.21/(.17)
$\hat{R}^2$	.54	.37
n	923	923

* $p < .05$ ** $p < .01$

Table A.2 The Effect of Head of Household's Unemployment and Family Finances on Voting in Presidential Elections, Cross-sectional Model 2 [a]

Variable	1956	1964	1968 [b]
Constant	.61/(.17)**	-1.14/(.21)**	.18/(.22)
Family finances better	.42/(.09)**	-.12/(.10)	-.30/(.10)**
Family finances worse	-.31/(.10**	-.02/(.14)	.30/(.13)*
Head currently unemployed	***	-.88/(.59)	.09/(.46)
Head unemployed last year	—[c]	-.58/(.29)*	-.23/(.33)
$\hat{R}^2$	.24	.40	.35
n	1266	1111	911

	1972	1980 [d]
Constant	.08/(.24)	.01/(.22)
Family finances better	.26/(.11)	-.21/(.12)*
Family finances worse	-.14/(.13)	.13/(.12)
Head currently unemployed	-.11/(.28)	-.40/(.29)
Head unemployed last year	-.48/(.17)**	-.26/(.17)
$\hat{R}^2$	.32	.34
n	827	877

a. Neither Cross-sectional Model 1 nor Model 2 was used to analyze voting in years in which longitudinal data were available, i.e., 1958, 1960, 1974, and 1976. The equations reported here and in all the tables which follow also specified the battery of social background variables described in appendix 2, but for the sake of brevity the estimates for these variables are not reported. b. Wallace voters were excluded from the analysis in 1968. c. The 1956 study did not ask respondents about any past unemployment suffered by their family head. d. Anderson voters were excluded from the analysis in 1980.
* $p < .05$ ** $p < .01$ *** Not included in the equation because of very low n.

Table A.3 The Effect of Head of Household's Unemployment and Family Finances on Voting in Congressional Elections, Cross-sectional Model 2

Variable	1956	1962	1964
Constant	.45/(.18)**	.23/(.24)	-1.03/(.23)**
Family finances better	.45/(.09)**	-.05/(.12)	-.08/(.11)
Family finances worse	-.23/(.12)*	.21/(.14)	-.12/(.15)
Head currently unemployed	***	-.25/(.38)	-.62/(.49)
Head unemployed last year	—ᵃ	-.10/(.22)	-.07/(.26)
$\hat{R}^2$	.31	.26	.34
n	1157	697	957

	1966	1968	1970
Constant	-.05/(.28)	-.11(.22)	-.51/(.28)*
Family finances better	-.20/(.13)	-.05/(.11)	.13/(.18)
Family finances worse	-.14/(.13)	.32/(.13)**	-.08/(.17)
Head currently unemployed	-.09/(.51)	-.57/(.50)	-.06/(.50)
Head unemployed last year	—ᵃ	-.50/(.36)	-.09/(.36)
$\hat{R}^2$	.27	.24	.21
n	677	871	683

a. The 1956 and 1966 studies did not ask respondents about any past unemployment suffered by their family head.
* $p < .05$ ** $p < .01$ *** Not included in the equation because of very low n.

Table A.3 The Effect of Head of Household's Unemployment and Family Finances on Voting in Congressional Elections, Model 2 *(cont.)*

Variable	1972	1978	1980
Constant	-.53/(.25)*	-.29/(.22)	-.32/(.21)
Family finances better	.19/(.12)	-.25/(.10)*	-.12/(.12)
Family finances worse	.01/(.14)	-.15/(.10)	.07/(.12)
Head currently unemployed	-.23/(.31)	-.20/(.32)	-.00/(.30)
Head unemployed last year	-.25/(.20)	-.07/(.15)	.13/(.16)
$\hat{R}^2$	.19	.25	.24
n	692	1009	859

* $p < .05$ ** $p < .01$

Table A.4 The Effect of Personal Economic Problems upon Voting in Presidential and Congressional Elections, 1972, Cross-sectional Model 2[a]

Variable	President	Congress
Constant	.15/(.24)	-.46/(.27)*
Family finances better	.26/(.11)**	.19/(.12)
Family finances worse	-.14/(.13)	.01/(.14)
Inflation	.09/(.15)	-.25/(.16)
Declining real income	-.23/(.23)	-.55/(.29)*
Unemployment related	-.52/(.30)*	-.1.16/(.44)**
Taxes	.13/(.21)	-.31/(.22)
General economic problems	-.01/(.14)	-.12/(.15)
$\hat{R}^2$	.22	.27
n	760	645

a. See note 17, chapter 5.
* $p < .05$ ** $p < .01$

Table A.5   National Economic Assessments and Voting:
Presidential Elections, Cross-sectional Model 2

Variable	1964	1968 [a]	1972 [b]	1980 [c]
Constant	-1.00/(.22)**	.22/(.23)	.11/(.24)	.08/(.26)
Personal economic experiences				
Family finances better	-.07/(.10)	-.26/(.11)**	.19/(.12)	-.23/(.13)*
Family finances worse	-.00/(.14)	.27/(.13)*	-.12/(.14)	.10/(.13)
Head unemployed currently	-.75/(.59)	.10/(.46)	—	-.44/(.30)
Head unemployed last year	-.59/(.30)*	-.28/(.35)	—	-.20/(.17)
Inflation	—	—	.08/(.15)	—
Declining real income	—	—	-.24/(.23)	—
Unemployment	—	—	-.48/(.30)	—
Taxes	—	—	.08/(.21)	—
General economic problems	—	—	.02/(.14)	—
National economic assessments				
Business conditions better	—	-.08/(.10)	.24/(.11)*	-.21/(.18)
Business conditions worse	—	.14/(.18)	-.30/(.10)*	.37/(.14)**
Unemployment	-.27/(.18)	.33/(.28)	-.13/(.21)	-.66/(.20)**
Inflation	.62/(.47)	.39/(.24)*	.02/(.14)	-.20/(.14)
Taxes	.32/(.19)*	.43/(.20)*	.42/(.25)*	.54/(.40)
More government programs	-.64/(.10)**	-.21/(.10)*	-.10/(.17)	-.58/(.20)**
Less government spending	.23/(.20)	.60/(.26)**	.05/(.30)	-.46/(.22)*
General economic problems	***	***	-.33/(.19)*	-.40/(.18)*
$\hat{R}^2$	.46	.38	.24	.40
n	1111	911	827	877

a. Wallace voters were excluded from the analysis in 1968. b. See note 16, chapter 6. c. Anderson voters were excluded from the analysis in 1980.
$p < .05$ ** $p < .01$ *** Not included in the equation because of very low *n*.

Table A.6   National Economic Assessments and Voting:
Congressional Elections, Cross-sectional Model 2

Variable	1962	1964	1966	1968
Constant	.27/(.24)	-.90/(.23)**	-.01/(.30)	-.12/(.23)
Personal economic experiences				
Family finances better	-.03/(.12)	-.06/(.11)	-.13/(.13)	-.02/(.11)
Family finances worse	.20/(.14)	-.12/(.15)	-.15/(.13)	.29/(.13)*
Head unemployed currently	-.24/(.38)	-.50/(.49)	-.16/(.52)	-.54/(.50)
Head unemployed last year	-.11/(.22)	-.06/(.26)	—	-.63/(.37)*
Inflation	—	—	—	—
Declining real income	—	—	—	—
Unemployment	—	—	—	—
Taxes	—	—	—	—
General economic problems	—	—	—	—
National economic assessments				
Business conditions better	-.15/(.12)	—	-.33/(.13)**	-.15/(.10)
Business conditions worse	-.01/(.14)	—	.00/(.14)	.10/(.17)
Unemployment	—	-.26/(.18)	.10/(.33)	.61/(.27)*
Inflation	—	1.06/(.55)*	.44/(.16)	.54/(.24)*
Taxes	—	-.34/(.11)*	.29/(.23)	.41/(.20)*
More government programs	—	.24/(.22)	-.03/(.15)	-.04/(.11)
Less government spending	—	.44/(.21)*	.41/(.19)*	.56/(.22)**
General economic problems	—	—	-.09/(.34)	—
$\hat{R}^2$	.26	.37	.31	.27
n	697	957	677	871

* $p < .05$ ** $p < .01$ *** Not included in the equation because of low *n*.

Table A.6   National Economic Assessments and Voting:
Congressional Elections, Cross-sectional Model 2 *(cont.)*

Variable	1970	1972	1978	1980
Constant	-.46/(.28)*	-.46/(.25)*	-.30/(.25)	-.13/(.26)
Personal economic experiences				
Family finances better	.15/(.18)	.16/(.12)	-.21/(.11)*	-.09/(.13)
Family finances worse	-.07/(.18)	.04/(.15)	-.15/(.11)	.06/(.12)
Head unemployed currently	-.12/(.50)	—	-.20/(.32)	.07/(.31)
Head unemployed last year	-.09/(.36)	—	-.09/(.15)	.19/(.17)
Inflation	—	-.19/(.17)	—	—
Declining real income	—	-.55/(.29)*	—	—
Unemployment	—	-1.12/(.44)**	—	—
Taxes	—	-.28/(.22)	—	—
General economic problems	—	-.10/(.15)	—	—
National economic assessments				
Business conditions better	—	.15/(.12)	-.16/(.11)	-.38/(.18)*
Business conditions worse	—	-.36/(.17)*	.06/(.11)	.04/(.13)
Unemployment	.01/(.20)	-.09/(.23)	-.46/(.27)*	-.59/(.19)**
Inflation	-.09/(.15)	-.23/(.15)	-.05/(.14)	-.29/(.14)*
Taxes	.20/(.25)	.10/(.25)	.04/(.24)	.49/(.38)
More government programs	-.22/(.14)*	-.13/(.17)	.31/(.25)	-.52/(.19)**
Less government spending	.27/(.35)	-.27/(.32)	.18/(.23)	-.11/(.22)
General economic problems	-.06/(.21)	-.21/(.20)	.12/(.19)	-.40/(.18)*
$\hat{R}^2$	.23	.27	.27	.28
n	683	692	1009	859

* $p < .05$ ** $p < .01$

Notes

Chapter 1

1. Hadley Cantril, *The Pattern of Human Concerns* (New Brunswick, New Jersey: Rutgers University Press, 1965).

2. The most notable of these is Edward R. Tufte, *Political Control of the Economy* (Princeton: Princeton University Press, 1978).

3. Data from these surveys were made available by the Inter-University Consortium for Political and Social Research. Neither the original collectors of the data nor the Consortium bear any responsibility for the analyses or interpretations presented here.

Chapter 2

1. Research in this area makes up one of the oldest quantitative traditions in political science. It provides considerable encouragement to the contemporary researcher, in that the crudeness of most of the analysis in this early work indicates that (at least in terms of statistical methodology) we have come a long way. For reviews of this literature see Gerald Kramer, "Short-Term Fluctuations in U.S. Voting Behavior, 1896-1964," *American Political Science Review* 65 (1971):131-43, or Kristen Monroe, "Econometric Analyses of Electoral Behavior: A Critical Review," *Political Behavior* 1 (1979):137-173.

2. Kramer, "Short-Term Fluctuations in U.S. Voting Behavior."

3. Anthony Downs, *An Economic Theory of Democracy* (New York: Harper, 1957).

4. Morris Fiorina, *Retrospective Voting in American National Elections* (New Haven: Yale University Press, 1981), p. 5.

5. For an early influential study of retrospective voting see V. O. Key's classic *The Responsible Electorate* (New York: Vintage, 1966). The most comprehensive theoretical and empirical work in this area, though, is Fiorina's *Retrospective Voting in American National Elections*. It should be noted that both Key and Fiorina assume retrospective voting is incumbency-oriented. This is not a logical necessity, however, as will be pointed out later in this chapter.

6. Fiorina, *Retrospective Voting*, p. 13; Samuel Popkin, John W. Gorman, Charles Phillips, and Jeffrey A. Smith, "Comment: What Have You Done for Me Lately? Toward An Investment Theory of Voting," *American Political Science Review* 70 (1976):779-805, p. 793.

7. Results of a study by Bloom and Price tend to support an asymmetric version of the hypothesis: congressional candidates of the incumbent president's party are punished for economic downturns—the worse the economy, the worse they do—but above a certain point they are not increasingly rewarded for higher levels of prosperity. Although this finding implies that incumbents live in an uncongenial political environment, it is probably still the case that they would prefer running for reelection during good times than during poor times. See Howard S. Bloom and H. Douglas Price, "Voter Response to Short-run Economic Conditions: The Asymmetric Effect of Prosperity and Recession," *American Political Science Review* 69 (1975):1240-54.

8. Although the explanatory power of different economic indicators varies considerably from study to study, the finding of a positive relationship between economic performance and electoral outcomes is quite robust, present in several different time series employing many different statistical models. Furthermore, strong evidence of this link has been found for presidential as well as congressional elections. For a large sample of research in this area see (besides Kramer's original 1971 article) Gerald H. Kramer and Susan Lepper, "Congressional Elections," in W. O. Aydelotte, ed., *Dimensions of Quantitative Research in History* (Princeton: Princeton University Press, 1972); Susan Lepper, "Voting Behavior and Aggregate Policy Targets," *Public Choice* 18 (1974):67-81; Edward R. Tufte, "Determinants of the Outcomes of Midterm Congressional Elections," *American Political Science Review* 69 (1975):812-26, and *Political Control of the Economy* (Princeton: Princeton University Press, 1978); Bloom and Price, "Voter Response to Short-run Economic Conditions;" Richard P. Y. Li, "Public Policy and Short-term Fluctuations in U.S. Voting Behavior: A Reformulation and Expansion," *Political Methodology* 3 (1976):49-70; and Ray C. Fair, "The Effect of Economic Events on Votes for President," *The Review of Economics and Statistics* 60 (1978):159-73.

There are analyses which challenge these findings, most notably George J. Stigler, "General Economic Conditions and National Elections," *American Economic Review* 63 (1973):160-7. He argues that, barring major economic disasters, fluctuations in general economic conditions have little systematic impact on congressional elections. Unlike other studies in this area, Stigler's measured economic conditions across the two-year period prior to elections instead of the one-year period used by nearly everyone else. This tends to "average-out" a great deal of economic change. Also, in his 1978 study Fair concluded that the electorate appears to consider economic trends in the year prior to the election at most. Thus, except for the length of the preelection period specified, the findings in this area are supportive of the hypothesis that the fortunes of the incumbent party depend, to a large degree, upon major economic trends.

9. Douglas A. Hibbs, "The Mass Public and Macroeconomic Policy: The Dynamics of Public Opinion Toward Unemployment and Inflation," *American Journal of Political Science* 23 (1979):705-31, p. 708.

10. Benjamin I. Page, "The Theory of Political Ambiguity," *American Political Science Review* 70 (1976):742-52.

11. Tufte, *Political Control of the Economy*, p. 74. Other observers have also concluded that in the United States parties make a great deal of difference in macroeconomic policymaking. See especially James L. Sundquist, *Politics and Policy: The Eisenhower, Kennedy, and Johnson Years* (Washington, D.C.: The Brookings Institution, 1969). Finally, journalistic accounts of presidential campaigns usually report finding differences in economic priorities expressed, if not with a great deal of clarity, in candidates' campaign rhetoric as well. See Theodore H. White, *The Making of the President, 1960* (New York: Atheneum Publishers, 1961); *The Making of the President, 1972* (New York: Atheneum Publishers, 1973). Also see Jules Witcover, *Marathon: The Pursuit of the Presidency, 1972-76* (New York: Viking Press, 1977).

12. Douglas A. Hibbs, "Political Parties and Macroeconomic Policy," *American Political Science Review* 71 (1977):1467-87.

13. Hibbs's analysis eschewed simple cross-time, cross-administration comparisons for precisely this reason. He instead opted for an "intervention analysis" technique developed by Box and Tiao, which, as he put it, permitted "estimation of the hypothesized effects of government macroeconomic policies on the unemployment rate, net of trends, cycles, and stochastic fluctuations in the unemployment time-series observations" ("Political Parties and Macroeconomic Policy," p. 1475). Although it is impossible to provide a very good explanation in so short a space, the basic idea behind the Box-Tiao model is to measure changes in either slope or intercept induced by a policy intervention off of a baseline, autoregressive-moving average series. For a detailed exposition of the technique see George E. P. Box and G. C. Tiao, "Intervention Analysis with Applications to Economic and Environmental Problems," *Journal of the American Statistical Association* 70 (1975):70-79. For a discussion of this and other standard techniques see Douglas A. Hibbs, "On Analyzing the Effects of Policy Interventions: Box-Jenkins and Box-Tiao vs. Structural Equation Models," in D. Heise, ed., *Sociological Methodology, 1977* (San Francisco: Jossey Bass, 1977), pp. 137-79.

14. Arthur M. Okun, "Comments on Stigler's Paper," *American Economic Review* 63 (1973):172-7.

15. This is especially true if incumbency-oriented voting and policy-oriented voting are both present and, perhaps, reinforcing each other. In this case voters would perceive the out-party as able to apply more effort and/or skill in precisely the problem area in which the incumbents' efforts had failed.

16. According to Downs's analysis, voters' aversion to uncertainty made it a dominant strategy for politicians, once elected, to do what they said they were going to do. See Downs, *An Economic Theory of Democracy*, pp. 103-9.

17. Okun, "Comments on Stigler's Paper." A similar argument is made by Douglas Rivers, who suspects that Carter tilted too far in his efforts to reduce inflation in 1980. Carter's shift in priorities, he believes, further weakened the partisan ties of many Democrats, who had long considered their party to be the "party of prosperity." See Douglas Rivers, "The Dynamics of Party Support in the American Electorate, 1952-1976," paper delivered at the 1980 annual meeting of the

American Political Science Association, Washington, D.C., August 28-31, 1980.

18. Saul Goodman and Gerald H. Kramer, "Comments on Arcelus and Meltzer: The Effect of Aggregate Economic Conditions on Congressional Elections," *American Political Science Review* 69 (1975):1255-65.

19. Allan H. Meltzer and Marc Vellrath, "The Effects of Economic Policies on Votes for the Presidency: Some Evidence from Recent Elections," *Journal of Law and Economics* 18 (1975):781-98.

20. Tufte, "Determinants of the Outcomes of Midterm Congressional Elections," p. 826.

21. Adam Smith, *The Theory of Moral Sentiments* (London: Henry G. Bohn, 1853).

22. Ron Kovic, *Born on the Fourth of July* (New York: McGraw-Hill, 1976).

23. Popkin et al., "What Have You Done for Me Lately?," p. 788.

24. Philip E. Converse, "Public Opinion and Voting Behavior," in Fred I. Greenstein and Nelson W. Polsby, eds., *Handbook of Political Science* vol. 4 (Reading, Mass: Addison-Wesley, 1975), p. 81.

25. Converse, "Public Opinion and Voting Behavior," p. 98.

26. Norman H. Nie, Sidney Verba, and John R. Petrocik, *The Changing American Voter* (Cambridge, Mass: Harvard University Press, 1976), p. 106.

27. Morris P. Fiorina, "Economic Retrospective Voting in American National Elections: A Micro-Analysis," *American Journal of Political Science* 22 (1978): 426-43; Ricardo Klorman, "Trend in Personal Finances and the Vote," *Public Opinion Quarterly* 42 (1978):31-48; Tufte, *Political Control of the Economy*; Donald R. Kinder and D. Roderick Kiewiet, "Sociotropic Politics: The American Case," *British Journal of Political Science* 11 (1981):129-61. These studies assessed the impact of voters' perceived financial situations only after controlling for their party identification in one way or another. Almost all survey analyses of voting behavior proceed in this manner, so assume, unless informed otherwise, that any such study discussed in this book includes partisanship controls.

28. Mikal Ben-Gera Logan, "Short-Term Economic Changes and Individual Voting Behavior," manuscript, Yale University, 1977; Fiorina, "Economic Retrospective Voting"; Donald R. Kinder and D. Roderick Kiewiet, "Economic Discontent and Political Behavior: The Role of Personal Grievances and Collective Economic Judgments in Congressional Voting," *American Journal of Political Science* 23 (1979):495-517.

29. Ben-Gera Logan, "Short-Term Economic Changes and Individual Voting Behavior"; Klorman, "Trends in Personal Finances and the Vote."

30. Some of the major works in this area include Richard R. Alford, *Party and Society: The Anglo-American Democracies* (Chicago: Rand McNally, 1963); Seymour M. Lipset and Stein Rokkan, eds., *Party Systems and Voter Alignments: Cross-National Perspectives* (New York: Free Press, 1967); Richard Rose, ed., *Electoral Behavior: A Comparative Handbook* (New York: Free Press, 1974).

31. Hibbs, "Political Parties and Macroeconomic Policy," p. 1470.

32. Frank Lerman, "Proto-Chapter 2," dissertation manuscript, Massachusetts Institute of Technology, 1978, p. 27.

33. Kay Schlozman and Sidney Verba, *Injury to Insult* (Cambridge, Mass.: Harvard University Press, 1979), pp. 204-5. It should be noted that the range of policy preferences which appeared to reflect personally experienced unemployment was tightly circumscribed. As they explained:

Thus, although unemployment seems to be related to views on economic policy, the relationship varies with the proximity of the issue in question to the specific needs and interests of the unemployed. On three items that have direct relevance to their jobless predicament, the unemployed have distinctive views. They are more likely than their working occupational counterparts to favor substantial efforts to end unemployment, to feel that the government should provide for those in need, and to accept a program of public employment for those out of work. When it comes to policies that are less immediately relevant to the special problems of the unemployed, such as redistribution of wealth by taxing the rich or limiting income, or to policies that advocate radical change as the price of reducing unemployment, ending capitalism or assigning jobs, the unemployed are less distinctive in their attitudes and the differences across occupational categories are considerably smaller.

34. D. Roderick Kiewiet and Donald R. Kinder, "Political Consequences of Economic Concerns—Personal and Collective," paper delivered at the annual meeting of the American Political Science Association, New York, New York, September, 1978; David O. Sears, Richard R. Lau, Tom Tyler, and Harris M. Allen, "Self-Interest vs. Symbolic Politics in Policy Attitudes and Presidential Voting," *American Political Science Review* 74 (1980):670-84.

35. Schlozman and Verba, *Injury to Insult*, p. 319. It should be noted that Kinder and Kiewiet also investigated the effect of personally experienced unemployment upon voting in congressional elections, but looked only at the incumbency-oriented hypothesis. Although they generally found little support for it, their analysis uncovered the same ambiguous finding in the 1976 congressional election, i.e., respondents whose head of household had recently been out of work gave more support than expected to Democratic candidates. See Kinder and Kiewiet, "Economic Discontent and Voting Behavior," p. 503.

36. Fiorina, *Retrospective Voting*, pp. 37-40.

37. David E. Repass, "Issue Salience and Party Choice," *American Political Science Review* 65(1971):389-400.

38. Arthur Miller and Warren Miller, "Partisanship and Performance: "Rational" Choice in the 1976 Presidential Election," paper presented at the 1977 annual meeting of the American Political Science Association, Washington, D.C., September 1977.

39. Kinder and Kiewiet, "Economic Discontent and Voting Behavior," p. 522.

40. Schlozman and Verba, *Injury to Insult*, p. 194.

41. Stanley Feldman, "Economic Self-Interest and Political Behavior," *American Journal of Political Science* 26 (1982):446-66.

42. Paul M. Sniderman and Richard A. Brody, "Coping: The Ethic of Self-Reliance," *American Journal of Political Science* 21 (1977): 501-21.

43. Schlozman and Verba, *Injury to Insult*, p. 200.

44. Kiewiet and Kinder, "Political Consequences of Economic Concerns," p. 48.

45. Logan, "Short-term Economic Changes and Individual Voting Behavior"; Kinder and Kiewiet, "Economic Discontent and Voting Behavior"; Morris P. Fiorina, "Short and Long-term Effects of Economic Conditions on Individual Voting Decisions," paper presented at the Second International Workshop of the Politics of Inflation, Unemployment, and Growth, University of Bonn, Bonn, West Germany, January, 1979.

46. Kinder and Kiewiet, "Economic Discontent and Voting Behavior"; Fiorina, *Retrospective Voting in American National Elections.*
47. Schlozman and Verba, *Injury to Insult,* p. 327.
48. Tufte, *Political Control of the Economy,* p. 85.

Chapter 3

1. This is essentially the approach taken by V. O. Key. His analyses, however, were based not upon longitudinal data, but upon voters' recall of how they had voted in the previous election. Unfortunately, a recent study by Niemi and his associates shows that such reports are full of errors and inconsistencies, making recall measures an extremely unreliable source of data. See V. O. Key, *The Responsible Electorate* (New York: Vintage, 1966); and Richard G. Niemi, Richard S. Katz, and David Newman, "Reconstructing Past Partisanship: The Failure of the Party Identification Recall Question," *American Journal of Political Science* 24 (1980):633-51.
2. The "previous election" refers to the previous congressional election if voting behavior in a congressional election is being predicted, the previous presidential election if a presidential election is being considered. In 1976, for example, the previous election was 1974 for the congressional vote, but 1972 for the presidential race.
3. The results of Fiorina's study are encouraging on this point. He found that correlations between indicators of economic conditions and concerns and noneconomic evaluations and issue positions, e.g. on civil rights and foreign policy, were extremely low. See Morris P. Fiorina, "Economic Retrospective Voting in American National Elections: A Micro-Analysis," *American Journal of Political Science* 22 (1978):426-43.
4. John E. Jackson, "Issues and Party Alignment," in L. Maisel and P. M. Sacks, eds., *The Future of Political Parties* (Beverly Hills: Sage, 1975), and Morris P. Fiorina, *Retrospective Voting in American National Elections* (New Haven: Yale University Press, 1981), p. 93.
5. Angus Campbell, Philip E. Converse, Warren E. Miller, and Donald E. Stokes, *The American Voter* (New York: Wiley, 1960).
6. Philip E. Converse, "The Nature of Belief Systems in Mass Publics," in David E. Apter, ed., *Ideology and Discontent* (Glencoe, Illinois: The Free Press, 1964); Philip E. Converse and Gregory B. Markus, "Plus ça Change . . .: The New CPS Election Study Panel," *American Political Science Review* 73 (1979):32-49.
7. Philip E. Converse, "The Concept of a Normal Vote," in Angus Campbell, Philip E. Converse, Warren E. Miller, and Donald E. Stokes, *Elections and the Political Order* (New York: Wiley, 1966).
8. Richard W. Boyd, "Popular Control of Public Policy: A Normal Vote Analysis of the 1968 Election," *American Political Science Review* 66 (1972): 429-49.
9. Kenneth J. Meier, "Party Identification and Vote Choice: The Causal Relationship," *Western Political Quarterly* 28 (1975):496-505.
10. Richard A. Brody, "Stability and Change in Party Identification: Presidential to Off-Years," paper delivered at the 1977 annual meeting of the American Political Science Association, Washington, D.C., September, 1977.
11. Brody, "Stability and Change in Party Identification."

12. Fiorina, *Retrospective Voting.*

13. Douglas Rivers, "The Dynamics of Party Support in the American Electorate, 1952-1976," paper delivered at the 1980 annual meeting of the American Political Science Association, Washington, D.C., August 28-31, 1980.

14. Benjamin I. Page and Calvin Jones, "Reciprocal Effects of Policy Preferences, Party Loyalties, and the Vote," *American Political Science Review* 73 (1979):1071-89.

15. W. Phillips Shively, "Information Costs and the Partisan Life Cycle," paper delivered at the 1977 annual meeting the the American Political Science Association, Washington, D.C., September, 1977.

Chapter 4

1. Steven J. Rosenstone, Raymond E. Wolfinger, and Richard A. McIntosh, "Voter Turnout in Midterm Elections," paper delivered at the 1978 annual meeting of the American Political Science Association, New York, New York, September, 1978.

2. Institute for Social Research, Survey Research Center, *A Panel Study of Income Dynamics* (Ann Arbor, Michigan: University of Michigan, 1972). High correlations between the aggregate average of the family finances item and several macroeconomic indicators also attest to its validity. Subtracting the percentage of respondents who reported being worse off from the percentage who said they were better off, Kinder and Kiewiet found there to be a -.68 correlation (Pearson *r*) between this figure and change in per capita real disposable income for the period 1956-1976. Klorman found the net percentage difference between the "worse off" and "better off" categories was also highly correlated with other macroeconomic indicators, including food and nonfood components of the consumer price index, change in short term interest rates, and the Commerce Department's index of coincident indicators. In short, all available evidence indicates that responses to this item do reflect individuals' recent economic fortunes. See Donald R. Kinder and D. Roderick Kiewiet, "Economic Discontent and Voting Behavior: The Role of Personal Grievances and Collective Economic Judgments in Congressional Voting," *American Journal of Political Science* 23 (1979):495-527, and Ricardo Klorman, "Trend in Personal Finances and the Vote," *Public Opinion Quarerly* 42 (1978):31-48.

3. Stanley Feldman, "Economic Self-Interest and Political Behavior," *American Journal of Political Science* 26 (1982):446-66.

4. Morris P. Fiorina, *Retrospective Voting in American National Elections* (New Haven: Yale University Press, 1981).

5. Kinder and Kiewiet, "Economic Discontent and Voting Behavior."

6. Although the rate at which voters discount past conditions and events may seem to be a fairly mundane empirical question, it actually has important theoretical implications. Certainly political business cycle theories, which posit that incumbents attempt to time peaks in economic activity to coincide with elections, depend upon voters having high discount rates for both past and future states.

7. Howard S. Bloom and H. Douglas Price, "Voter Response to Short-run Economic Conditions: The Asymmetric Effect of Prosperity and Recession," *American Political Science Review* 69 (1975):1240-54.

8. M. Stephen Weatherford, "Economic Conditions and Electoral Outcomes:

Class Differences in the Political Response to Recession, *American Journal of Political Science* 22 (1978):917-38.

9. Gerald H. Kramer, "Aggregate Data Versus Survey Research Findings on the Effects of Economic Conditions on Voting Behavior: Which Ones Should We Believe? Or Is There Really Any Discrepancy?" Paper delivered at the 1981 annual meeting of the Public Choice Society, New Orleans, Louisiana, March, 1981.

10. David O. Sears and Richard R. Lau, "Inducing Apparently Self-interested Political Preferences," *American Journal of Political Science* 27 (1983):forthcoming.

11. Although this point should probably have been made earlier, the dummy variables used in this analysis reflect unemployment suffered by voters' heads of household because all members of a family whose chief breadwinner has been out of work are usually directly and adversely affected. However, about 60% of the respondents in the CPS National Election Studies are head of their household (they are so counted if they are single). Furthermore, substitution of the head of household unemployment terms with ones which instead register respondents' past and current unemployment produces similar but slightly weaker estimates.

12. Arthur M. Okun, "Comments on Stigler's Paper," *American Economic Review* 63 (1973):172-7.

13. Ray C. Fair, "The Effect of Economic Events on Votes for President," *The Review of Economics and Statistics* 60 (1978):159-73.

14. Sam Kernell, "Explaining Presidential Popularity," *American Political Science Review* 72 (1978):506-22.

15. That differences in the order of the questionnaire items from year to year did not perturb results of the present analysis does not mean that Sears and Lau have not diagnosed a potentially serious problem. They have. The evidence they present, however, suggests that the biggest problems posed by item order differences do not come in observing relationships between personal economic fortunes and vote reports, but rather in the relationships between personal economic fortunes and attitudinal reports, e.g., presidential approval or job performance ratings. See Sears and Lau, "Inducing Apparently Self-interested Political Preferences."

16. This statistic is an estimate of R^2 (the percent of variance explained) derived from the unobserved regression postulated by the assumptions of the probit model. See Richard D. McKelvey and W. Zavoina, "A Statistical Model for the Analysis of Ordinal Level Dependent Variables," *Journal of Mathematical Sociology* 4 (1975):103-20.

17. As indicated earlier, change in per capita real disposable income generally out-performs other macroeconomic indicators in predicting aggregate vote totals in congressional elections. Thus it would seem smarter simply to ask respondents whether *their* incomes had gone up or down in the previous year instead of whether they and their family were worse off or better off. The CPS National Election Studies of 1962, 1966, 1968, and 1972 did ask this question. Kinder and Kiewiet combined this income change item and the family finances item into a simple additive index, but found the index did no better in predicting voting than the family finances item used alone. Fiorina, furthermore, found the simple bivariate relationship between voting in congressional and presidential elections and the income change item was even weaker than that between voting and the family finances item. See Kinder and Kiewiet, "Economic Discontent and Voting Behavior," and Fiorina, *Retrospective Voting*, p. 29.

Chapter 5

1. Robert E. Hall, "The Nature and Measurement of Unemployment," National Bureau of Economic Research Working Paper 252, July 1978; Paul Osterman, "Understanding Youth Unemployment," *Working Papers for a New Society* 6 (1978):58-63.

2. The staff at CPS was extremely accommodating and helped make the task of recoding the interviews much less arduous than it might have been. I would like to thank Warren Miller for his approval of the project, and Ann Robinson, Alice Hayes, and Maria Sanchez for their valuable assistance.

3. The 1972 and 1974 studies followed up the personal problem question by asking, "Of all you've told me, what would you say is the *single most* important problem you face?" Determining the economic problem deemed most important was thus straightforward: if the answer to the question was an economic problem, it was selected; if not, and the other problem coded was economic, the latter was selected as the most important economic problem. In 1976 no follow-up questions were included in the survey. Over 70% of the respondents who cited an economic problem mentioned only one. Some, however, did mention two problems. Usually the one deemed most important could be inferred from the respondent's remarks. On the occasions in which it could not, the first problem mentioned was chosen.

4. David Cameron, "Economic Inequality in the United States," manuscript, Yale University, 1979.

5. Douglas A. Hibbs, "The Mass Public and Macroeconomic Performance: The Dynamics of Public Opinion Toward Unemployment and Inflation," *American Journal of Political Science* 23 (1979):705-31.

6. George Katona, *Psychological Economics* (New York: Elsevier, 1975).

7. Katona, *Psychological Economics*; Arthur Okun, "Inflation: Its Mechanics and Welfare Costs," *Brookings Papers on Economic Activity*, 1975, pp. 351-90.

8. In fact, the more surprising thing about the individuals who said that their worst personal economic problem was a declining real income may be that 24% of them claimed that their family's financial situation had actually improved over the previous year. Although this pattern of responses is a little unusual, there is no reason to believe that they were misreporting. Evaluations of one's economic well-being, after all, depend on many other things in addition to real income. An individual who was being hurt by a declining real income, for example, might still feel better off financially than a year ago if at that time he or she had been beset by major unexpected expenses.

9. These findings are virtually identical to Katona's. He found that individuals' responses to a question asking how badly they were being hurt by inflation—much, a little, or not at all—had little correlation with their income level. See Katona, *Psychological Economics*.

10. Douglas A. Hibbs, "Political Parties and Macroeconomic Policy," *American Political Science Review* 71 (1977):1467-87.

11. Hibbs, "The Mass Public and Macroeconomic Performance."

12. In a similar analysis of public opinion toward inflation in Great Britain, Alt found that respondents' preferences for various anti-inflationary policies—more taxation, more unemployment, strict wage controls, or less government spending—were related in a complicated though reasonable way to their economic and demographic characteristics. Consistent with the interpretation

being proffered here, Alt also reasoned that the pattern of responses he observed was produced by a relatively uniform aversion to inflation, but differential amounts of aversion to the various types of bitter anti-inflationary medicine. See James E. Alt, *The Politics of Economic Decline* (Cambridge, U. K.: Cambridge University Press, 1979).

13. David Piachaud, "Inflation and Income Distribution," in Fred Hirsch and John H. Goldthorpe, eds., *The Political Economy of Inflation* (Cambridge, Massachusetts: Harvard University Press, 1978). See also G. L. Bach and James B. Stephenson, "Inflation and the Redistribution of Wealth," *Review of Economics and Statistics* 61 (1974):1-13; and Alan S. Blinder and Howard Y. Esaki, "Macroeconomic Activity and Income Distribution in the Post-War United States," *Review of Economics and Statistics* 60 (1978):604-9.

14. It has been argued, of course, that inflation is a problem *only* when it is unanticipated, and that a world in which the inflation rate were a steady, fully anticipated 10% per annum would be as predictable and secure as a world with stable prices. According to Okun, however, the goal of "steady inflation" is a "mirage." As he put it:

> The main problem of steady inflation as a goal is its lack of credibility. Targetting on a stable first derivative is admitting failure in the effort to stabilize the level. Why should anyone expect any greater success in stabilizing the rate of change of the price level than in stabilizing the price level?

See Okun, "Inflation: Its Mechanics and Welfare Costs," p. 385.

15. Nick Vasilatos and Douglas A. Hibbs, "Public Opinion Toward Unemployment and Inflation in the United States, 1970-76," unpublished technical report, 1977.

16. Thurow makes this point in his recent book. See Lester C. Thurow, *The Zero-Sum Society* (New York: Basic Books, 1980).

17. Because of a number of constraints, the 1972 CPS National Election Study was divided into two parts—Form I and Form II. Although most questions were included in both forms, many appeared on only one form or the other. As it has for virtually all previous multivariate analyses using this data set, this leads to unresolvable problems for the present study. In this case, the family finances item appeared on Form I, but the personal problems question battery was placed on Form II. It was thus impossible to include both sets of indicators in the same equation.

However, substituting the personal economic problem dummies (specified in the equations reported in tables 5.3 and 5.4) for the head of household unemployment measures (specified in the equations reported in tables 4.1 and 4.2) had virtually no effect upon estimates of the family finances terms in the 1974 and 1976 elections equations. More precisely, two pairs of probit estimates were identical, three differed by .01, and the difference between the remaining pair was .04. Because of this it was decided to run the probit equations for the 1972 elections with the Form II data (i.e., the personal economic problem dummies), and simply to report the estimates for the family finances terms which had been generated in the previous analysis (wherein the head of household unemployment terms had been specified).

18. An alternative explanation for why voters who felt their worst personal economic problem was inflation supported Nixon so strongly in 1972 is that they felt he had done well on the inflation front. Although the 1972 CPS survey did not include any questions which might have brought some evidence to bear on this matter, polls taken at that time by Market Opinion Research certainly did not support this interpretation. These data indicated that people's perceptions of how well Nixon had dealt with inflation were not all that favorable. It seems quite likely, then, that the effect registered by this estimate was more anti-McGovern than it was pro-Nixon. See Frederick T. Steeper and Robert M. Teeter, "Comment on 'A Majority Party in Disarray'," *American Political Science Review* 70 (976):806-13.

19. Converse has given such responses the moniker of "nonattitudes," which, in analyses insensitive to this problem, can erroneously be inferred to have large effect upon voting. See Philip E. Converse, "Attitudes and Non-attitudes: Continuation of a Dialogue," in Edward R. Tufte, ed., *The Quantitative Analysis of Social Problems* (Reading, Massachusetts: Addison-Wesley Publishing, 1970).

20. A classic example of this was the Vietnam War issue in the 1968 presidential campaign. See Benjamin I. Page and Richard A. Brody, "Policy Voting and the Electoral Process: The Vietnam War Issue," *American Political Science Review* 66 (1972):979-97.

21. Page and Jones's analysis clearly identifies the problems inherent in using "issue proximity" measures to predict voting behavior. See Benjamin I. Page and Calvin Jones, "Reciprocal Effects of Policy Preference, Party Loyalties, and the Vote," *American Political Science Review* 73 (1979):1071-89.

22. Benjamin I. Page, *Choices and Echoes in Presidential Elections* (Chicago: University of Chicago Press, 1978).

23. In recent years several researchers have attempted to deal with this problem through the use of nonrecursive, simultaneous equation systems. Although this approach is certainly promising, these methods have not been used extensively enough in public opinion and voting research to permit any firm conclusions about their utility. It seems doubtful that they are going to be a panacea, however, in that most of the serious measurement problems inherent in survey research remain. The main emphasis of the present study's estimation strategy, of course, is to employ measures of the independent variables which are as resistant to projection and rationalization as possible.

For important examples of simultaneous equation models applied to voting behavior see John Jackson, "Issues, Party Choices and Presidential Votes," *American Journal of Political Science* 19 (1975):163; Page and Jones, "Reciprocal Effects of Policy Preferences, Party Loyalties and the Vote"; Gregory Markus and Philip E. Converse, "A Dynamic Simultaneous Equation Model of the Electoral Choice," *American Political Science Review* 73 (1979):1055-70.

24. Table 5.5 is based upon the 1976 sample. These same relationships between respondents' partisanship and their personal economic problems, however, were evident in the 1972 and 1974 samples as well.

25. Kay Schlozman and Sidney Verba, *Injury to Insult* (Cambridge, Masss: Harvard University Press, 1979).

26. The percentage of heads of household who had been out of work in the previous year was a little lower—about 15% in all three waves of the study.

27. The CPS surveys failed to ascertain whether the unemployed were receiving compensation or not, and available data allow only rough estimates of the extent of coverage. Eighty percent of the labor force is covered by unemployment insurance, but the unemployed come disproportionately from that segment of the labor force which is not covered. Cameron estimates that the percentage of the unemployed actually receiving compensation ranges from 40 to 65%, depending upon where the economy is in the business cycle. It is also true, though, that heads of household are more likely to be eligible for benefits than are members of the labor force in general. So a large majority of the unemployed heads of household in the CPS surveys probably were receiving compensation, but an exact figure cannot be deduced. See Cameron, "Economic Inequality in the United States."

28. Donald R. Kinder and D. Roderick Kiewiet, "Economic Discontent and Political Behavior: The Role of Personal Grievances and Collective Economic Judgments in Congressional Voting," *American Journal of Political Science* 23 (1979):495-527; Paul M. Sniderman and Richard A. Brody, "Coping: The Ethic of Self-Reliance," *American Journal of Political Science* 21 (1977):501-21; Richard A. Brody and Paul M. Sniderman, "From Life Space to Polling Place: The Relevance of Personal Concerns for Voting Behavior," *British Journal of Political Science* 7 (1977):337-60.

29. The argument here is that the more universalistically people view the nature of their problems, the more likely they are to hold the government responsible for alleviating them. The data here and in Sniderman and Brody's study certainly indicate that this is a reasonable generalization. Quite likely, however, people also respond politically to more selective policies (e.g., which affect them in their roles as air traffic controllers, dairy farmers, or machinists laid off upon cancellation of the B-1 bomber project) but which also have a readily apparent impact upon their personal well-being. A conventional survey of a representative cross-section of the adult population of the United States, however, will simply not pick up enough individuals from such selective groups to permit analysis of their voting decisions.

30. Stanley Feldman, "Economic Self-Interest and Political Behavior," *American Journal of Political Science* 26 (1982):446-66.

31. On the other hand, simply believing that the government should provide assistance with one's economic problems does not automatically make these problems relevant to voting decisions. After all, social security payments, welfare benefits, unemployment compensation, and rent subsidies are supplied bureaucratically by particular government agencies, and there is no reason why recipients of these benefits need associate them with with the actions of incumbent politicians. All in all, though, the potential influence of personal economic problems upon decisions is undoubtedly greater when individuals believe their problems warrant governmental assistance than when they believe they should handle their problems on their own.

32. It seems surprising that anyone would name taxes their worst economic problem and *not* believe that the government should assist them. After all, government is the only institution which levies taxes, and thus the only one which can reduce them. What is probably the case, though, is that many respondents simply failed to imagine any assistance on taxes coming from the government, given that it is government which is the source of their problem. To some extent this argument may also apply to concerns over inflation.

33. The findings here seem compatible with the results of Schlozman and Verba's far more extensive study of the unemployed. They concluded that although most jobless respondents believed they themselves were primarily responsible for either coping with unemployment or finding a new job, most also felt that the government should provide them with some assistance. See Schlozman and Verba, *Injury to Insult*.

34. Popkin and his associates' study, however, provides some additional confidence that this finding is genuine. Data from Cambridge Survey Research polls taken in 1972 indicated that ratings of McGovern's competence in a wide range of issue areas were considerably more unfavorable than respective ratings of the Democratic party. See Samuel Popkin, John W. Gorman, Charles Phillips, and Jeffrey A. Smith, "Comment: What Have You Done for Me Lately: Toward an Investment Theory of Voting," *American Political Science Review* 70 (1976): 779-805.

35. While the evidence in table 5.8 certainly supports this claim, it does so only indirectly. The cross-tabulation was based upon all respondents, not just voters, and a direct test would require a probit analysis specifying the appropriate interaction terms, i.e. problem cited x perceived government responsibility x perceived party differences. Unfortunately, there are far too few cases available to inspire any confidence in the results of such an analysis (assuming it was even possible to compute the probit estimates). In this case it seems more reasonable to make inferences upon indirect evidence and (barely) sufficient *n*, rather than upon a more direct test involving a hopelessly small number of cases.

Chapter 6

1. Donald R. Kinder and D. Roderick Kiewiet, "Economic Discontent and Political Behavior: The Role of Personal Grievances and Collective Economic Judgments in Congressional Voting," *American Journal of Political Science* 23 (1979):495-517.

2. Mikal Ben-Gera Logan, "Short-Term Economic Changes and Individual Voting Behavior," manuscript, Yale University, 1977; Morris P. Fiorina, "Short and Long-Term Effects of Economic Conditions on Individual Voting Decisions," in Douglas A. Hibbs and Heino Fassbender, eds., *Contemporary Political Economy* (Amsterdam: North-Holland Publishing Company, 1981), pp. 73-100.

3. Edward R. Tufte, *Political Control of the Economy* (Princeton: Princeton University Press, 1978), p. 85; Kay Schlozman and Sidney Verba, *Injury to Insult* (Cambridge, Massachusetts: Harvard University Press, 1979), p. 327.

4. In all studies except 1958, respondents were subsequently asked which of the problems they had mentioned they considered most important. The CPS coders were thus able to order problem reports according to perceived importance, and the highest ranking economic problem (if any were mentioned) was included in table 6.1. The procedure followed in the 1958 study was a little more complicated. After respondents were asked whether they thought "problems here at home in the United States" had gotten better in the past year, gotten worse, or stayed the same, they were asked to report the particular problems they had in mind. Only the reported problems of those who believed things had stayed the same or had worsened were coded, but about 85% of the sample fell into these two categories. As table 6.1 indicates, inflation and unemployment were the only two economic

problems which could be extracted from the CPS codes for that year. The "no problem mentioned" category is inordinately large in 1958 because responses relating to defense and foreign affairs were inappropriate, and because it includes the 15% who felt the U.S. domestic situation had been improving.

5. Analyzing the aversion of various population subgroups to inflation relative to unemployment from 1971 through 1976, Hibbs concluded that "popular aversion to inflation versus unemployment is sensitive to the *level* unemployment experience of *particular groups* and to *changes* in the unemployment rate prevailing in the *macroeconomy*." On the other hand, opinion appeared to be sensitive only to the rate of inflation, and not to changes in the rate. See Douglas A. Hibbs, "The Mass Public and Macroeconomic Performance: The Dynamics of Public Opinion Toward Unemployment and Inflation," *American Journal of Political Science* 23 (1979):705-31.

For an excellent study of public reaction to inflation, unemployment, and other economic ills in Great Britain, see James E. Alt, *The Politics of Economic Decline* (Cambridge, U. K.: Cambridge University Press, 1979). One of the major strengths of Alt's study is his intensive investigation of the formation of economic expectations.

6. David E. Repass, "Issue Salience and Party Choice," *American Political Science Review* 65 (1971):389-400; Arthur Miller and Warren Miller, "Partisanship and Performance: "Rational" Choice in the 1976 Presidential Election," paper presented at the 1977 annual meeting of the American Political Science Association, September, 1977, Washington, D.C..

7. The coding scheme displayed in table 6.1 was constructed from the myriad of categories supplied by the CPS. Its unemployment category, and thus the one used in this analysis, contained individuals who believed that the government should create more jobs, expand retraining programs, and provide aid to depressed areas—responses which could legitimately fall under the heading of "need more government programs." Although it is a judgment call, the coding scheme thus attaches more importance to their substantive concern over unemployment than to their favoring more public spending to remedy it. Perusal of the verbatim interview transcripts, furthermore, indicates that most remarks which fell into the category were one simple word—"unemployment"—with no further elaboration.

8. Contrary to Wagner's "law," Wildavsky contends that the demand for social welfare benefits and other public services is greater when the economy is performing poorly. Cameron's study of eighteen advanced industrialized democracies found that expansion of their public sectors was inversely related to the rate of economic growth, and thus favored Wildavsky. Whether or not this expansion occurs in response to popular demand, however, is hard to say. It could well be that legislation mandating unemployment insurance and other countercyclical aid tends to be enacted during periods of prosperity. At any rate, the data in table 6.1 give no clear clues as to the relationship between the performance of the economy and the demand for public services. It appears that the percentage of people citing the need for more government programs is larger during prosperous years, but complaints about government spending and taxes seem to be somewhat more frequent in good years as well. See Adolph Wagner, "The Nature of the Fiscal Economy," in Richard A. Musgrave and Alan T. Peacock, eds., *Classics in the Theory of Public Finance* (London: MacMillan, 1958); Aaron Wildavsky, *Budgeting: A Comparative Theory of Budgetary Processes* (Boston: Little, Brown, 1975); and

David R. Cameron, "The Expansion of the Public Economy," *American Political Science Review* 72 (1978):1243-61.

9. Cameron, "The Expansion of the Public Economy."

10. Tufte, *Political Control of the Economy*, pp. 97-100.

11. Kinder and Kiewiet, "Economic Discontent and Political Behavior."

12. David O. Sears, Thomas R. Tyler, Jack C. Citrin, and Donald R. Kinder, "Political System Support and Public Response to the Energy Crisis," *American Journal of Political Science* 22 (1978):56-82; Richard Lau, Thad Brown, and David O. Sears, "Self-interest and Civilians' Attitudes Toward Vietnam," *Public Opinion Quarterly* 42 (1978):464-83; and John B. McConahay and William D. Hawley, "Is it the Buses or the Blacks?" paper delivered at the 1977 annual meeting of the American Psychological Association, August 1977, San Francisco, California.

13. This analysis is based upon McKelvey and Zavoina's generalization of the probit model to *n*-chotomous ordinal variables. See Richard McKelvey and William Zavoina, "A Statistical Model for the Analysis of Ordinal Level Dependent Variables," *Journal of Mathematical Sociology* 4 (1975):103-20.

14. The actual wording of this question was as follows:

We'd like to know how people are affected financially by inflation these days. Would you say that you (and your family living here) have been *badly hurt* by inflation, *hurt somewhat, not affected* very much, or *helped* financially by inflation?

The dummy variables here were formed by the 20% of respondents who claimed to have been badly hurt and by the 17% who said that inflation had either not affected them or had helped them (only 2% gave the latter answer).

Given that this question directly asked respondents about the impact inflation had had upon them personally, an obvious thing to do would be to include the resultant dummy variables in the voting analyses. When added to the equations reported in chapter 4 and later on in this chapter, however, the effects associated with these variables were very close to zero. It would be rash, though, to conclude much from these results. They are confined to one election year, and the lack of effects may be due to question wording as much as anything else. It could well be that questions asking respondents *how* badly they have been hurt are less reliable than the other types of questions used in this study.

15. The problem in the 1962 study is just the opposite—in that year the CPS survey included the national business conditions question but not the most important national problem question. It is extremely doubtful, however, that either inflation or unemployment dominated public concern in this relatively prosperous year, and so estimates of the business conditions terms should not be much affected by the omission of the national economic problem dummies.

16. As in the previous analysis, the results for 1972 were actually derived from separate analyses of variables from Form I (the family finances and national business conditions terms) and Form II (the personal and national economic problem batteries) and so should be regarded with some caution. Analyses in the previous chapter (see note 17, chapter 5) and the findings reported in table 6.4, however, provide assurance that the estimates reported in tables 6.5 and 6.6 would not have been a great deal different had responses to these questions been available for all members of the 1972 sample.

17. Kinder and Kiewiet, "Economic Discontent and Political Behavior"; Ben-Gera Logan, "Short-Term Economic Changes and Individual Voting Behavior"; Fiorina, "Short and Long-Term Effects of Economic Conditions on Individual Voting Decisions."

18. These findings are strongly corroborated by Converse, Clausen, and Miller's analysis of the 1964 election. Although relying upon different sets of survey measures, they too concluded that most voters were not at all sympathetic to Goldwater's views concerning the proper size and scope of the public sector, and that despite his generally unfavorable image, the election was much more a repudiation of Goldwater's policy proposals than of Goldwater himself. See Philip E. Converse, Aage Clausen, and Warren E. Miller, "Electoral Myth and Reality: The 1964 Election," *American Political Science Review* 59 (1965):321-36.

19. Benjamin I. Page and Richard A. Brody, "Policy-Voting and the Electoral Process: The Vietnam War Issue," *American Political Science Review* 66 (1972): 979-97.

20. Philip E. Converse, Warren E. Miller, Jerrold G. Ruske, and A. C. Wolfe, "Continuity and Change in American Politics: Parties and Issues in the 1968 Elections," *American Political Science Review* 63 (1969):1083-105.

21. William Safire, *Safire's Political Dictionary* (New York: Random House, 1978).

22. Paul M. Sniderman and Richard A. Brody, "Coping: The Ethic of Self-Reliance," *American Journal of Political Science* 21 (1977):501-11; Richard Brody and Paul M. Sniderman, "From Life Space to Polling Place: The Relevance of Personal Concerns for Voting Behavior," *British Journal of Political Science* 7 (1977): 337-60.

23. The actual question wording in the 1960, 1964, and 1968 studies was:

> Which party do you think would be most likely to do what you want on this problem, the Democrats, the Republicans, or wouldn't there be any difference between them?

This question was posed to respondents after each particular problem they mentioned. Up to three problems per respondent were coded, so the *n* in these years (which is based upon the number of responses) is larger than the number of respondents. In 1972 the question was worded a little differently:

> Which political party do you think would be most likely to get the government to be helpful on this problem?

In 1976 and 1980 the wording was also slightly different:

> Which political party do you think would be most likely to get the government to do a better job in dealing with this problem—the Democrats, the Republicans, or wouldn't there be any difference between them?

In these studies the party differences questions were asked only in regard to what respondents had cited as the single most important problem, so only one response per respondent is available. Finally, in 1972 only half the respondents in the survey were asked the battery of national problems questions.

24. James E. Alt, *The Politics of Economic Decline* (Cambridge, U. K.: Cambridge University Press, 1979), pp. 235-48.

25. Ivor Crewe, James E. Alt, and Bo Särlvik, "The Erosion of Partisanship in Britain, 1964-74," paper presented at the meeting of the Political Studies Association, 1976.

Chapter 8

1. Thomas E. Mann and Raymond E. Wolfinger, "Candidates and Parties in Congressional Elections," *American Political Science Review* 74 (1980):617-32.

2. Donald R. Kinder and D. Roderick Kiewiet, "Sociotropic Politics: The American Case," *British Journal of Political Science* 11 (1981):129-61, p. 145.

3. Gary C. Jacobson, "The Effects of Campaign Spending in Congressional Elections," *American Political Science Review* 72 (1978):469-91.

4. Morris P. Fiorina, "Economic Retrospective Voting in American National Elections: A Micro-Analysis," *American Journal of Political Science* 22 (1978): 426-43, p. 440.

5. Gary C. Jacobson and Samuel Kernell, *Strategy and Choice in Congressional Elections* (New Haven: Yale University Press, 1981).

6. It should also be noted that the mass and elite phenomena are not mutually exclusive. Democratic candidates in 1974, for example, probably did not spend all their campaign money advertising their irresistable personal characteristics; they surely used at least some of the funds in their larger-than-average campaign chests to remind voters about how badly the Republicans had screwed up the economy. I would like to thank Roger Noll for this observation.

7. Alexis de Tocqueville, *Democracy in America* (Garden City, New York: Doubleday, 1969), pp. 235-6.

8. As indicated earlier, Jacobson and Kernell's recent book thoroughly examines elite reactions to economic conditions. The most thorough individual-level study of the effects of economic conditions upon voter turnout—a subject which this book has largely ignored—is that by Rosenstone. He found, among other things, that personal economic adversity significantly depresses the probability that a given individual will show up at the polls. See Steven J. Rosenstone, "Economic Adversity and Voter Turnout," manuscript, Yale University, 1980.

9. When growth or income terms are not specified, it is generally an unemployment measure which then becomes the most powerful explanatory variable. This is about what should be expected, though, given that the correlation between changes in real income and the unemployment rate is very high (usually the Pearson r is between -.8 and -.9). See Arthur M. Okun, "Comments on Stigler's Paper," *America Economic Review* 63 (1973):172-7; Ray C. Fair, "The Effect of Economic Events on Votes for President," *Review of Economics and Statistics* 60 (1978):159-73; Bruno S. Frey and Friederich Schneider, "Recent Research on Empirical Politico-Economic Models," in Douglas A. Hibbs and Heino Fassbender, eds., *Contemporary Political Economy* (Amsterdam: North-Holland Publishing Company, 1981), p 17.

10. Donald R. Kinder and D. Roderick Kiewiet, "Economic Discontent and Political Behavior: The Role of Personal Grievances and Collective Economic Judgments in Congressional Voting," *American Journal of Political Science* 23 (1979):495-527, p. 500.

11. Saul Goodman and Gerald H. Kramer, "Comment on Arcelus and Meltzer: The Effect of Aggregate Economic Conditions on Congressional Elections," *American Political Science Review* 69 (1975):1255-65; Allan H. Meltzer and Marc Vellrath, "The Effect of Economic Policies on Votes for the Presidency: Some Evidence from Recent Elections," *Journal of Law and Economics* 18 (1975):781-98. It should be noted that a later, corrected version of Kramer's original 1971 article did find an incumbency-oriented effect associated with inflation. See Gerald H. Kramer, "Short-Term Fluctuations in U.S. Voting Behavior, 1896-1964," *Bobbs-Merrill Reprint Series in Political Science*, no. 68877.

12. David Piachaud, "Inflation and the Income Distribution," in Fred Hirsch and John H. Goldthorpe, eds., *The Political Economy of Inflation* (Cambridge, Massachusetts: Harvard University Press, 1978), p. 115.

13. Douglas A. Hibbs, "The Mass Public and Macroeconomic Performance: The Dynamics of Public Opinion Toward Unemployment and Inflation," *American Journal of Political Science* 23 (1979):705-31, p. 728.

Appendix 1

1. John Aldrich and Charles F. Cnudde, "Probing the Bounds of Conventional Wisdom: A Comparison of Regression, Probit, and Discriminant Analysis," *American Journal of Political Science* 19 (1975):571-608, p. 586.

2. David J. Finney, *Probit Analysis* (Cambridge, U.K.: Cambridge University Press, 1971).

3. Aldrich and Cnudde, "Probing the Bounds of Conventional Wisdom."

Index